Embracing the Mystery

Embracing the Mystery

Prayerful Responses to AIDS

EDITED BY
SEBASTIAN SANDYS

First published in Great Britain 1992
SPCK
Holy Trinity Church
Marylebone Road
London NW1 4DU

British Library Cataloguing in Publication Data

A catalogue record for this book is available from the British Library

ISBN 0-281-04574-7

Typeset by Rowland Phototypesetting Ltd
Bury St Edmunds, Suffolk
Printed in Great Britain by
BPCC Hazells Ltd
Aylesbury, Bucks

In loving memory of Stephen Philip Davis

The Mystery

The meaning of things, and their purpose,
Is in part now hidden
But shall in the end become clear.
The choice is between
The Mystery and the absurd.

To embrace the Mystery
Is to discover the real.
It is to walk towards the light,
To glimpse the morning star,
To catch sight from time to time
Of what is truly real.

It is no more than a flicker of light
Through the cloud of unknowing,
A fitful ray of light
That is a messenger from the sun
Which is hidden from your gaze.
You see the light but not the sun.

When you set yourself to look more closely,
You will begin to see some sense
In the darkness that surrounds you.
Your eyes will begin to pick out
The shape of things and persons around you.
You will begin to see in them
The presence of the One
Who gives them meaning and purpose,
And that it is He
Who is the explanation of them all.

Cardinal Basil Hume OSB

Contents

Preface

We are in a time of crisis. AIDS and HIV have claimed the lives of thousands of people in our country and many hundreds of thousands elsewhere. As so often at these times many people turn to God, in anger, in confusion or in helplessness. As individuals and as community we seek understanding, explanations, healing and above all love. This book does not seek to provide these things but I hope it contains some tools for the task. Although some of the meditations were not written specifically as a response to AIDS, they have proved helpful to me and I hope they will to you.

This book is no panacea. It is not an escape from the hurt. I hope it can be a resource for those seeking God in this tragedy. It is I suppose a collection of signposts. As we learn to live with AIDS and HIV we can rediscover God, and the love that is intertwined with our sorrow and anger.

Many of the people who have written for this book are living daily with the nightmare that has become reality in the lives of so many. These are people who in the midst of all the pain that AIDS brings have found themselves closer to God and supported by the love they find.

I hope this collection will be used by individuals as they pray but more importantly by communities who pray together.

My thanks are due to many more people than I can name but to Sara Maitland, Eva Heyman and Kate Gibbs go my special thanks. As to the people I have known whose lives with the virus have shown such charity and courage, my debt is beyond words.

Sebastian Sandys
August 1991

Dear Tom,

Thank you for your letter. You have asked of me a hard thing: to help you equate the despair and bewilderment you feel at the discovery that you now have full-blown AIDS with my belief in the loving purpose of God. You word it with admirable bluntness: 'Tell me how to find God in my illness', you ask. 'Tell me what it means to pray, or how prayer can help at such a time. Tell me, if there is a God, where he has gone. Tell me why I should matter to him, and what is the point of my life. And tell me what I can do with my overwhelming feelings of anger and guilt, frustration and loss.'

I want to reply with equal honesty, avoiding the glib, conventional phrases with which we professionals sometimes seek to protect ourselves; and in forcing me to write it down you are helping me to rediscover what lies at *my* centre, those resources which I too shall one day have to call on in the face of my own dying, whatever form that takes.

You begin by asking me how you can pray, but I can't answer that without affirming what I believe about God; and (equally important) what I don't believe. And to do so out of the mystery of our shared humanity. For unless we can share our vulnerability, and the few insights we may have garnered from our experience of the dark, we human beings aren't much help to each other. You don't have to live long to know what it's like to be a lonely, hurting human being, naturally frightened of pain and dying, and needing to be comforted and encouraged. And when it comes to AIDS, too often churches have been correctly perceived to be judgemental and exclusive, rather than open and affirming places.

Martin Luther once wrote that 'Christ's proper work is

to declare the grace of God, to console and to enlighten'. I'm not sure which is the more striking fact about Jesus' relationships with people: his tender cherishing of individuals (Mary Magdalene, Levi, Zacchaeus, the adulterous woman, the paralyzed man — the gospels are full of them), or his fierce refusal to discriminate between people on any grounds whatever, even seeking out those who were marginalized or considered ritually unclean. (They crucified him in the end for that.) Jesus knows that, whether they recognize it or not, each is hungry for the love of God, each made in his image, each needing to be consoled, forgiven, liberated from false ideas of God, and so 'enlivened' — with new hope, fresh life, breathed into them. The life of Christ, culminating in his death and resurrection, are seen as the start of a new creation: a wholly new relationship is established between the creative power who is Love and his creatures, in which pain and suffering remain a central and still mysterious part of living, but a relationship which will transcend death itself.

It doesn't feel like that most of the time. Certainly not when you are diminished by illness in every part of you: body, mind and spirit. And I hear the desperation in your words: 'How can I pray, or even believe in a loving God, at such a time as this?'

One of the best essays in a recent book on AIDS, *Embracing the Chaos* (SPCK 1990), that by Peter Baelz, former Dean of Durham, was placed last. Yet it asked the questions that have to precede all the rest: What sort of world is it in which we live? and, What sort of God is it in whom we put our trust and hope? To see your illness (as you might be tempted to) as in any sense a punishment, an affliction sent by God, is to misunderstand both the mechanics of creation and the nature of the creator. Just as the concept of freedom is implicit in any loving relationship, so the world of nature has a freedom which we experience as chance and unpredictability. Accidents, illness, earthquakes, are random and unpredictable events. Yet they occur within a framework of determined and determining laws. Theologians and philosophers will argue the *why?* of this mystery till the cows come home. I'm simply concerned to state it and then move from it to the perceived nature of that more profound mystery, whom we call God.

The central paradox in the Christian belief about God is that he is invisible but not inscrutable, beyond his universe, yet discovered within it. God is beyond our imagining (which arouses in us wonder), yet chooses to reveal himself (which moves us to respond with love). He is not a force of unchanging and unchangeable power, but with us at the very heart of his world. As St John puts it: 'No one has ever seen God; it is the only Son, who is close to the Father's heart, who has made him known.' Made him known in the only terms we can understand: in *our* terms, as a loving, vulnerable, suffering human being. 'God doesn't give an answer to our questions', writes the liberation theologian, Leonardo Boff, 'but in Jesus God enters into the heart of the questions.'

This belief that God is Christlike at once rules out alternative views of God as uncaring, removed from our suffering and completely unknowable. It is to trust that undergirding this chancy creation there lies the force of self-giving love; that it has this quite other dimension where spirit relates to spirit (or even Spirit). I'm not taking off into some cloud-cuckoo-land. Those who give and receive love are no strangers to that dimension.

Yet love, which as those who now love you know only too well, costs us dear. It is at root a giving of yourself to another, *come what may*. It is therefore quite often a kind of dying. It demands loyalty and sacrifice, and it may well encompass much pain and even death. Indeed, for God, a

3

cross. What the cross of Christ shows is that our pain and anguish are known intimately to God himself, and that the presence of Jesus once in history was the presence of God as he has always been and always will be. A friend of mine has written that 'the crucified Jesus is the only accurate picture of God the world has ever seen'; and from his condemned cell in a Nazi concentration camp in 1944 Dietrich Bonhoeffer could write: 'Only a suffering God can help.'

Europe faced a similar crisis to AIDS when, in the sixteenth century, syphilis spread through the population. In the museum at Colmar is the famous Isenheim altarpiece by Grunewald, where the tortured figure of Christ on his cross is covered with syphilitic sores. It is believed the altar-piece was painted for a hospital for terminal syphilitic patients, so its message is clear: Christ's suffering (and, by implication, his resurrection) touches and interpenetrates all suffering, and no one is excluded from the love of the merciful and humble God revealed in Jesus. Either God was not in Christ and the cross is the symbol of all that is destructive and ultimately meaningless; or God was in Christ and the cross is the ultimate word of a God who shares your pain and your loneliness and weakness, even the frightening sense of outrage and bewilderment you may feel in the face of death. ('My God, my God, why hast thou forsaken me?') And who dies, his body racked, his side pierced; and is placed in his grave. But the God who has the power to create and give life has the power to re-create it, and God shows in the resurrection of Jesus that his purpose in creating us for union with himself is not to be frustrated even by death. He can and will clothe us with a new body. For the first disciples, the resurrection of Jesus is the final proof that everything he had said about the Father's love was true, yet he still bore the marks of the nails in his hands and the spear in his side. Jesus did not offer people perfect health or a painless death. What he offers is life of a new quality: a new relationship with God of such a quality that nothing that may happen to us can destroy it.

'If there is a God, where has he gone?' you ask. To a much lesser extent than you, I know the feeling and I've said the same words. And I can only reply, out of my own small experience of a diminishing and drawn-out illness: 'However hard it is to grasp, the extraordinary truth is that the God revealed in Christ is here. Not far off and indifferent. Once he was made flesh like you, and now at every moment he is for you, and with you, and indeed within you; his love manifested in the friend or lover going through this experience with you.' To put it in a sentence: the lover's words 'I love you because you are you', words that affirm our infinite value to each other, are also the words of God in Christ to each one of us. This is what 'consoles and enlivens': not the threat of judgement, but the assurance that, feeble and distraught as you may now *feel*, you need not doubt that you are loved, loved in your life and loved through and beyond your death.

So, Tom, if you will accept that this (however clumsily and inadequately) points to truths about the nature of the world and the nature of God, what does it imply about the meaning of your illness? First, that it is a consequence, not a punishment. Secondly, that it is possible to use your illness, even your dying, to discover your meaning and, paradoxically, your true value. For what dictates the *quality* of your life is to know yourself loved, and that truth transcends your physical condition. To maintain some sense of control and self-esteem in the face of chaos and uncertainty will in itself be to live creatively; but you can go even further. The question isn't whether you are scared or feel guilty or angry, but what you *do* with those feelings.

Life is about making choices: between one action and

another, between generous self-giving and a more selfish holding back; and it is also about what we make of the harsh, unlooked-for blows, sickness and death and grief. Last autumn a close friend of mine died of a pretty rapid cancer. When it was first diagnosed he asked in some agony of spirit: 'Do I fight this – or do I accept it as a gift?' The word was a startling one, yet the fact is that, when his illness was clearly terminal, he could begin to see his dying as part and parcel of the gift that is life and react to what seemed so destructive by drawing some good out of it. He found even in the anguish of losing his life that kind of confidence and trust in God, an assurance that his life had meaning and still had meaning, for he was (and always would be) of value to God, his family and his friends. He came to believe that every scrap of his life, however fleeting, was of untold value to God. And by believing that he demonstrated the real triumph of the human spirit.

You have asked me what form your prayer might take and how it could help you live and die creatively. Prayer isn't magic. Nor is it a way of twisting God's arm. Prayer is about attuning yourself to the love of God, who wills all that is good for you, but it does not override the progress of the cancer cell or the AIDS virus. The philosopher John Macmurray once wrote:

> The maxim of illusory religion runs: 'Fear not; trust in God and he will see that none of the things you fear will happen to you'; that of real religion, on the contrary, is: 'Fear not, the things that you are afraid of are quite likely to happen to you, but they are nothing to be afraid of.'

Prayer is about achieving that kind of trust. It has to do with your inward journey and your present sense of incompleteness, your ability as a human being made in God's image to be open to the one who gave you your

6

present earthly life which is now being slowly withdrawn. The life of God himself is within you now, and you cannot ever be out of his presence, even if you experience this presence as absence — as most of us do most of the time. There will be days — weeks, perhaps — when you will be so diminished, or feel so cheap, that you can't pray at all. Then you must let others hold you in the presence of God.

I pray because God *is*. And I try to sit, kneel, lie, stand before him as I am, seeking to be open, recalling the gift (of my life and my loves, of himself in Christ), affirming who I am and his life within me. Being open means being honest about how I feel, being able to give him my boredom or pain or confusion. If at times of extremity I need to shout or swear at God I can do so, knowing that God alone can absorb (did absorb once on Calvary) every bit of anger or resentment I want to throw at him, every wound I inflict on myself or others, everything that stems from my hurt and damaged self. That he can take it, and take it away by forgiving me.

I use the psalms if I want to link my feelings to those of the ancient Jewish people and so to the prayers of Jesus. How many Jews must have prayed the psalms in Belsen and Auschwitz, many of them gut-cries of desolation, even despair:

> Why do you stand so far off, O Lord?
> why do you hide your face in time of need? (Psalm 10.1)

> The waves of death encompass me,
> and the floods of chaos overwhelm me . . .

> In my anguish I called to the Lord,
> I cried for help from my God. (Psalm 18. 4, 6: Alternative Service Book version)

And for a sense of despair and isolation, read Psalm 88 in the Book of Common Prayer:

7

O Lord God of my salvation, I have cried day and night before thee:
O let my prayer enter into thy presence, incline thine ear unto my calling.

For my soul is full of trouble
and my life draweth nigh unto hell . . .

Thou has laid me in the lowest pit:
in a place of darkness, and in the deep . . .

Thou hast put away mine acquaintance far from me:
and made me to be abhorred of them . . .

Unto thee have I cried, O Lord:
and early shall my prayer come before thee.

Lord, why abhorrest thou my soul:
and hidest thou thy face from me?

My lovers and friends hast thou put away from me:
and hid mine acquaintance out of my sight.

But they lead on, time and again, to words of reassurance, even thanksgiving. The very next psalm begins:

My song shall be always of the loving-kindness of the Lord . . .

One of the greatest of the psalms is 139:

Not a word comes from my lips
but you, O God, have heard it already.

You are in front of me and you are behind me,
you have laid your hand on my shoulder . . .

Where shall I go from your Spirit,
where shall I flee from your Presence?

If I climb to the heavens you are there;
if I descend to the depths of the earth, you are there also . . .

If I should cry to the darkness to cover me,
and the night to enclose me,

the darkness is no darkness to you,
and the night is as clear as the day. (Translation by Jim
Cotter)

So be honest. But, first and last in so far as you can, be
still. 'Nothing in creation is so like God as stillness', wrote
a great fourteenth-century German mystic. Different
things can help induce a stilling of our thoughts: certain
kinds of music, or the contemplating of a natural object, or
the slow repetition of a phrase. (There will be suggestions
in later chapters.) And, if you can, be thankful. Not
thankful that you are ill and weak, but thankful for every
act of love you receive, and thankful for the opportunity to
discover in your need and your anguish (I speak foolishly
and with great hesitation) something of your true value
and the meaning of your life.

Embracing the Chaos includes the story of Lloyd, who
died of AIDS two or three years ago. A close friend
describes how his illness gave Lloyd time for reflection
and a new awareness of the true value of small, everyday
things, incidents and relationships: how he made the most
of the 'present moment'. Because AIDS is a death-
threatening crisis, each day could be the last day, and your
whole perspective of what is important changes. Philip
Toynbee, when he was dying of cancer, wrote in his diary:

On my walk I stopped several times and looked at a
single tree as I haven't done for years. No; as I've never
done in my life before. The tree was there and now, in
its own immediate and peculiar right: *that* tree and no
other. And I was acutely here and now as I stared at it,
unhampered by past or future.

One of the greatest teachers on prayer, an eighteenth-century French priest called Jean-Pierre de Caussade, based his teaching on what he called 'the sacrament of the present moment'. His starting point is simple: God is love, and he is loving us at every instant of our lives, and can no more stop loving us than the sun can stop radiating heat. It follows that God's love is coming to us through each sinful moment, whatever it contains. We don't realize it because a) we're too active and b) we've not been taught to think like this. But perhaps the enforced passivity of illness can be used to help discover it; for no doubt the value we put on the events and relationships of each day is in inverse proportion to our life expectancy.

I have tried to suggest what it might mean for you to pray, and how prayer (how you relate to God) can help you. Nothing can help you more to use your illness creatively than if you can learn to live in the present moment. To ask forgiveness for whatever disturbs you from the past; and then let it be. Not to be anxious about the future, which is out of your hands. And to be able to do this not because, ostrich-like, you stick your head in the sand, but because what is true of God's love for you and your value in his sight is true at this and every other moment of your life. 'How is it', asks Soren Kierkegaard, 'that Christ managed to live without anxiety for the next day' when he must have known from the beginning of his public ministry that his life would not be long? It was, he says, because 'he had eternity with him in the day that is called today, hence the next day had no power over him, it had no existence for him'.

Well, there it is, Tom, for what it's worth. I offer you my words, but I ask you to forgive their inadequacy to convey the powerful truths I believe them to contain. Most language is banal in the face of suffering and dying. It was Flaubert who wrote that 'human language is like a cracked kettle on which we beat our tunes for bears to dance to, when all the time we are longing to move the stars to pity'. But love, when it is costly and unsentimental, is never banal. And I hope you will have the gift of love to take you through the rest of your earthly life, and beyond it.

Yours ever,

Michael Mayne
Dean of Westminster

PART ONE

'Why have you forsaken me?'

Psalm 22

1 My God my God   why have | you for | saken me:
   why are you so far from helping me
   and from the | words | of my | groaning?

2 My God I cry to you by day   but you | do not
   | answer:
   and by night | also · I | take no | rest.

3 But you con | tinue | holy:
   you that | are the | praise of | Israel.

4 In you our | fathers | trusted:
   they | trusted · and | you de | livered them;

5 to you they cried and | they were | saved:
   they put their trust in you | and were |
   not con | founded.

6 But as for me   I am a worm and | no | man:
   the scorn of | men · and de | spised · by the
   | people.

7 All those that see me | laugh me · to | scorn:
   they shoot out their lips at me and | wag their |
   heads | saying,

8 'He trusted in the Lord | let him · de | liver him:
   let him de | liver him · if | he de | lights in him.'

9 But you are he that took me | out of · the | womb:
   that brought me to lie at | peace · on my |
   mother's | breast.

10 On you have I been cast | since my | birth:
   you are my God | even · from my | mother's
   | womb.

11 O go not from me   for trouble is | hard at | hand:
   and | there is | none to | help.

12 Many [|] oxen · sur [|] round me:
    fat bulls of Bashan close me [|] in on [|] every [|] side.

13 They gape [|] wide their [|] mouths at me:
    like [|] lions · that [|] roar and [|] rend.

14 I am poured out like water
    and all my bones are [|] out of [|] joint:
      my heart within my [|] breast · is like [|] melting
  [|] wax.

15 My mouth is dried [|] up · like a [|] potsherd:
    and my [|] tongue [|] clings · to my [|] gums.

16 My hands and my [|] feet are [|] withered:
    and you [|] lay me · in the [|] dust of [|] death.

17 For many dogs are [|] come a [|] bout me:
    and a band of evil [|] doers [|] hem me [|] in.

18 I can count [|] all my [|] bones:
    they stand [|] staring · and [|] gazing · up [|] on me.

19 They part my [|] garments · a [|] mong them:
    and cast [|] lots [|] for my [|] clothing.

20 O Lord do not [|] stand far [|] off:
    you are my helper   [|] hasten [|] to my [|] aid.

21 Deliver my [|] body · from the [|] sword:
    my [|] life · from the [|] power · of the [|] dogs;

22 O save me from the [|] lion's [|] mouth:
    and my afflicted soul from the [|] horns · of the [|]
    wild [|] oxen.

The Alternative Service Book 1980

In bleak despair

A version of Psalm 88

*Refrain: There is drought in the depths of my being,
no rain, no water, no life.*

The praise of your salvation, O God,
has died on lips that are parched.
The story of your wonders towards us
has turned hollow, bitter, and sour.
I doubt any prayer can enter your heart,
your ear is deaf to my cry.

Soul-deep I am full of troubles,
and my life draws near to the grave.
I totter on the edge of the abyss,
ghostly, ghastly, shrivelled.
I am like the wounded in war that stagger;
like a corpse strewn out on the battlefield.

I belong no more to my people,
I am cut off from your presence, O God.
You have put me in the lowest of dungeons,
in a pit of scurrying rats.
To a wall that drips with water I am chained,
my feet sink into mud.

I feel nothing but a pounding in my head,
surges of pain overwhelm me.
I cannot endure this suffering,
this furious onslaught, so searing.
I can remember no time without terror,
without turmoil and trouble of mind.

I have been dying since the day of my birth:
O God, have I ever really existed?
I have never known who I am,
and even my friends who once loved me,
who gave me some sense of belonging,
have drawn back in horror and left me.

My sight fails me because of my trouble;
there is no light in the place of deep dark.
I am alone, bewildered, and lost;
yet I cannot abandon you, God.
Day after day I cry out to you,
early in the morning I pray in your absence.

Do you work wonders among the tombs?
Shall the dead rise up and praise you?
Will your loving kindness reach to the grave,
your faithfulness to the place of destruction?
Are the stories of old an illusion?
Will you again do what is right in the land?

*In times of despair, O God, rain showers of gentleness upon us,
that we may be kindly one to another and also to ourselves.
Renew in us the spirit of hope. Even in the depths of the darkness,
may we hear the approach of the One who harrows hell and
greets even Judas with a kiss.*

Jim Cotter

Living the Passion

A latter-day St Matthew's Passion.

I

> And he came up to Jesus at once and said,
> 'Hail Master!' And he kissed him. (26.49)

I remember the garden very well. I do not know why it should be this garden that comes to mind. This night garden which hid him in its shadows. Why him? Why should he return? Why him particularly, to be shuttled between self-pity and the apportioning of blame? I play on him day after day in the dark. This friend, coming like a stranger in the dark to me then.

I remember we leant over a broken wall. We looked out over the lights below. The city a mass of lights. No noise. No traffic. No life apart from we two there. He, and I. I did not know myself there in that strange place. I do not know myself now. Not here in this dark and this cold. Perhaps that is why he is returning. To watch with me.

I could not see his face as he came through the trees. An old garden. Abandoned. The green-houses shattered. He scrunched the broken glass under his brutal shoes. He came and leant on the wall and we looked down on the city. Yes. I remember we looked down on the city, on the streets and the blocks and the thousand lights. He moved closer. He lit his own light and I saw his mouth. It did not smile. It was a line across his chin. It was shut. It would open for the cigarette, then close. He breathed smoke gently.

When he came to me, I could smell the smoke and the leather of his jacket and the cold of the night. I could feel

19

the hardness of his body. His body was a body like my body. His lips were strange. All the way through I was conscious of his lips. I keep wondering if it was his kisses that betrayed me.

II

> And behold, one of those who were with Jesus stretched out his sword . . . (26.51)
> Then all the disciples forsook him and fled. (26.56)

When I first began to get tired, I was very angry. I was so angry my energy must have wasted in fuelling the rage. I would get ready to go to a club and be exhausted by the time I was dressed. I would take my clothes off and go to bed. Sometimes I would sit in a chair and think of the times when I had danced until morning. I would sit and think rampant sex thoughts. As if sex was a weapon, some defence. I wanted to escape into more and more sex. I was alone and afraid.

There is no escape and nobody comes. Hardly anybody. People just forgot me. It was nothing dramatic. They were always polite when I phoned. Always polite and always busy. I was too tired to get about much myself. They were frightened, I suppose. I just stayed in. Always exhausted. Always alone. I heard about the world and watched it on a screen.

Some weeks I would get to work. Some days I would battle to the office. I would be so drained that I had to get a taxi back home straight away. They wrote to me and asked me not to come. I stayed home. There was no one to touch. No one to be close to. Nobody phoned — almost as if they could catch something down the wires.

One night I had a dream. I remember this dream very well. I dreamt that they came down and painted a big red cross on my door. All across the door. Sometimes at night,

I see the red cross across the door and it feels as if the cross is daubed down my body now. All down my body. I remember that when the kissing was over, I realized how empty the garden was.

III

'I do not know the man.' (26.74)

It has always been a struggle facing up to who I am. There has always been a battle to gain some sense of pride in myself. Well, not even pride, just a sense of identity that was not hateful to myself. It took me years to believe I was a man. That sounds silly, but it did. Other guys in school were eager to start shaving. They would boast about all the changes happening to them. They were crazy about becoming men. When they used to show themselves in the changing rooms, I looked away in disgust. At least, I told myself it was disgust. Now I know it was self-loathing. I spent three weeks getting it together to buy a razor. I hated what I could not control in myself. I would not recognize the power of sex. I did not want to be set apart.

Funny, years on now, I thought I had myself worked out. I thought I was at peace with myself. I was glad to be a man with other men. I was gay. G.A.Y. I went to workshops and learned to shout it, 'G.A.Y.!' Self acceptance and all that.

When I read about the gay plague, all the self-loathing returned. It was always there. And there I was, timid and afraid, crouching behind a glass sea wall from the storm of abuse and lies. Hiding, shivering, believing every bad and hateful lie about myself. Denying myself again. Strange, how when one hates oneself, one believes every untruth they tell. As if I was an addict for self-degradation, lapping up punishment like a dog.

My brother came to see me. We were never very close. I

guess he never had any problem shaving. He took a day off work and came to see me. He sat by my bed, gave me a paper and some grapes. He was very awkward. When I told him, he did not look at me. He just got up and walked out. I watched him go. I saw the nursing sister speak to him. 'Ah, Mr Smith — about your brother . . . ' He stared at her, amazed. 'My brother? There must be some mistake. I do not know the man.'

IV

And they bound him and led him away and delivered him. (27.2)

I got pneumonia first. I became very ill and hot. I wanted to get some air. I was wandering around the corridor outside the flat, not knowing who I was. So they tell me. One of the neighbours met me. She called the ambulance.

That was my first time ever in an ambulance. They are vehicles one never expects to get inside. I have seen them in the street often, from the outside. I could never see inside. There is always blue glass, or sometimes it is brown, and there is no way of looking. Sometimes I have noticed forms moving behind the glass. Or I have made out shapes: the shapes of old people sitting in a line leaning on their frames, or with their sticks between their knees.

There was one line with their backs to me. One line facing them. They did not look out. I could not look in. They looked at each other, those two lines, and were not part of my world.

None of this is part of my world. Not the bed, nor the room, nor the ambulance. Particularly the ambulance — that first medical smell, its alien light, the surge of its engine.

They carried me from my flat like I was dead. They put me on a bed and carried me and I looked about me and saw the house from that strange angle and suddenly became so afraid.

Everything is slipping away. The ground is slipping away and I am falling into a great void. I have no control. I lie on a bed and am carried through my life and I watch it seep away. Everything familiar is falling away. I do not set the clock. I do not dial the phone or open doors. I do not choose my clothes. I do not take them off. I do not cook my food. I do not clean myself. I do not flush the toilet. I just lie here day after day becoming less and less. Other people do everything for me. I just lie here and let them.

V

'Are you the King of the Jews?' Jesus said, 'You have said so.' (26.59–68; 27.11–14)

I remember all those days of tests. One test after another. Shoving and pushing and jabbing and extracting. And all the questions. The morning after I had been brought in a doctor came to see me. It was a woman doctor. She was quite young — looked very tired. I felt rather sorry for her, though really I should have been feeling sorry for myself. Before she spoke, she read the charts at the bottom of my bed. She asked me straight out. She said, 'Are you a homosexual?'

Strange. I felt as though my life hung on my answer to that question. I wasn't sure how to make a reply. I was lying on the bed like this, flat out, helpless. She only wanted me to say yes or no. But I had no power over that word 'homosexual'. I have no power to define myself. I am all the names that people pin on me: Queer. Bender. Bandit. Bummer. Child molester. Poof. Fag. Nancy. Pervert. Deviant. Sick. Abnormal. Homosexual.

'If that's how you'd like to think of me,' I said.

23

She put the charts back and walked away.

In the paper I read two reports on 'homosexuals'. One said that we should be locked away. We are a danger to civilized society. The other was from a churchman. He said I deserve to die because of who I am.

VI

'Whom do you want me to release for you?' (27.15–23)

When I was waiting for the results of the tests, it never seriously occurred to me they might be positive. It had never occurred that one day it might be ME. Nobody imagines that they will die. Not really. Not young people. Not someone like me. I sat on the bed imagining what they might be doing, putting little bits of me in tubes and shaking them up, whizzing them round, smearing them about. Distasteful little bits of me, gazed and gazed at, charted, discussed, disputed over.

No way could it be me. Not me. Somebody else perhaps. Somebody sordid and stupid but not me. I had always been so clean and fit and well. In the gym, I would pump the machines like the others. So strong! At the pool, racing up and down the water, pushing my way through the water. Forcing it away from my face, surging toward the wall, heaving a turn. Then on, on, as if there was no end to my power.

Sometimes I am so tired I can barely reach for my cup. It spills all over me. It is heavy. I find it hard to grip now. Hard to direct my limbs where I want them to be. Sometimes, my body does not obey me. Nothing happens like it used to. Nothing works like it should. Except fear. Fear comes just the same.

When I think of how it used to be, I feel very angry. I hate the people who come to nurse me. I hate them because they can do for me what I would do for myself. I hate myself because of the way I am. Somebody else should be lying here, not me.

VII

'Why, what evil has he done?' (27.23)

Yesterday, I sat in the chair by my bed. I had a rug over my knees and I could see out of the window. Outside there is a car park and a rose bed and a scrappy piece of lawn. Just more hospital buildings beyond. I do not look out much. The curtains are drawn and it is light. Then it is dark and the curtains are drawn again. This happens every day. Every day the same, with a little bit more struggle.

I sat in the chair and looked at the floor. I looked at a tile for a long time. It is a pale blue and there is a dark blue blot running across it, like marble. I followed the line of the blot for a long while. I know that particular tile. I can pick it out from all the tiles now, and I follow its line. It is the line of a beach I was on once in Greece. It is the line of the blue sea lapping at the shore. I run to the line in my mind and feel the warmth of the sea creep up my legs and round my waist and I remember that once I was happy and free. I believed that everything was working for me.

If there is a God like they say there is, then God must have made that blue line in Greece. He must have put me here to watch it now. Here in this room. He must hate me. My father hated me, when he realized who I am. God hates me too for that perhaps. But what did I ever do for them to hate me, except to be myself?

VIII

He took water and washed his hands before the crowd. (27.24–5)

They took what they needed and found out what they wanted to know. They knew for days and days before they told me anything. They left me to lie in ignorance. When I asked the nurses, they glibly said that everything would be all right, and to rest. Eventually a doctor came and told me that I had pneumonia. He was very young and very sincere and full of the confidence of his science. But he found it hard to look into my eyes for long.

He took some more blood from my arm. He was very careful about injecting me. He put on opaque plastic gloves before he picked up the syringe. He ripped them off very quickly afterwards and slung them in a bin which the nurse took away. I watched him scrubbing his hands at the sink. Scrubbing and scrubbing, working so hard to wash something away. As if my blood was on his hands.

My blood is living death. Nobody wants to touch my blood for fear of becoming me — this wasting, shrinking, mangled stretch of flesh that is me. Some people will not touch me. Porters refused to move me once, even to touch my bed. Some nurses will not deal with my room. Some doctors wear masks. Being near me is dangerous. There is no one near me. No one to touch and be gentle with. No one to kiss. I am slowly ceasing to be human. I am alone, rotting on the edge of the world.

IX

He handed him over to be crucified. (27.26, 31)

They have not told me I am going to die, but I know that I will. Quite soon. They treat each new illness as best they can, but I am dying. There is no cure and therefore no hope. I know I am dying.

I struggle every day to do what I can, but they do most of it for me now. My body has unlearned every process that was taught it. I wake up in the stench of my own waste, like a baby. Sometimes I cry and cry because I am so frustrated and ashamed. There is nothing heroic or holy about it.

There are no special paths to be taken, no choices to be made. I am dying, disintegrating, splurting out and rotting away. It is just a battle for control. I lose and lose and lose. I am defeated. I am helpless. I am alone. I smell. I ache. I can do nothing.

That is what dying is.

Before, when I was on a ward, men used to die. We were not allowed to see them dead. Nothing was said about them dying. It was as though they had never been there. The man two beds up from me died. He died in the night when we were asleep. In the morning the curtains were drawn around him. There was always the same procedure. The men came from the morgue. They drew the curtains round all of us. They put screens across the aisle of the ward. I heard them wheel the trolley in, and heave the one two three body to its top. They brought him down with a thud. They sighed. They wheeled him away. They pulled the curtains back and the sick in the beds looked across at each other. Then they carried on reading their papers.

I have listened to that thud time and time in my mind. I know that when I make that thud, I shall be dead. Then this will be over.

X

And they stripped him and put a scarlet robe upon him.
(27.27–31)

They moved me to a special ward. It was a room with four beds. When I got there I knew that there was no future. It was a special ward. I watched a man come through the door. He was a tall man in a dressing gown and slippers. He wheeled a drip beside him as he shuffled along. The drip was of clear liquid in a bag. Sometimes he would lean on the stand and catch breath. I should say he had been a strong man once, an ideal man. He was big and dark. He had a fine moustache. He had been a proud man, though he had withered now. His muscles had waned. Skin sagged on his face.

I imagined him as he had been — taut and vital and full of power. I could see this man as he had been in the clubs and pubs. I saw him through imagined crowds, singularly sexual. Such vigour seemed like a mockery of him now as he struggled to his bed.

At his bedside, he took off his robe. His back was broad. A tube from the bag went into his arm. All across his body were patches of coloured skin. Scarlet-purple patches, all over.

XI

This man they compelled to carry his cross. (27.32)

I'm not sure how Simon heard that I was ill. He came to see me. He brought me some flowers. When he came into my room he kissed me. He came over to the bed and pulled me up from the sheet and put his arm around my shoulder and kissed my head. I felt like me again. He did not stay very long. When he was gone, I knew I was me and that I was good. That there was some good in me. Though my body has gone bad, I am good.

Sometimes I lie here and I wish I could get up and begin again. I wish I could get out where Simon is and live again. If I could have all my chances once again, it would be different. There would be no hurt or lies or pain this time. No dishonesty, no abuse. When I think like that I feel such pain inside. Such knotted pain. It drives out tears that sting. There is nothing I can do now. There are no means of amends.

Simon brought me daffodils. I watched them for hours and hours, until they died. Their white roots, their green, their yellow heads turn brown and dry. As a child, I would pick daffodils out in the garden for my mother. I would dip my finger deep down into the grass to pick them long, from the roots. When I gave them to my mother, she would smile. She would put them in a vase and admire them. I was happy then, to have made her smile with my daffodils. If only I could tell her I remember happy times — that they make me glad. If only I could pick her daffodils again. That would ease the years of silence and of crying.

XII

'My God, my God, why hast thou forsaken me?'
(27.33–50)

When they give me the injections, I look into their eyes to see if it is something different. Something that will bring on the end. I used to want that, when I realised that the end was going to come. I didn't know what it would be like. I didn't realise it would be this dribbling away, this half-life, this grinding down.

What I cannot bear is my mind raking over the rubbish of my life, hauling up scraps from the past, releasing the stench of deep buried sores. Then the anguish of being alone is the worst pain. Sorting the unspeakable debris alone. They do everything for me, but they do not clear this refuse from my head. No space to cherish what has been beautiful and fun.

There are red painted lines along my body. From the roots of my hair to my toes. From one hand to the other. A great red cross that is in me. All over me.

If there is a God then he must be like my father, like the headmaster, like the politician, the churchman. God must be like them to let me lie in such squalor alone. To let me stumble through the unresolved like this. To let the bad get the better of the good. If God is there, he sees the

worst, like they did. He doesn't accept any part of me.
Basically, God just isn't on my side.

Mark Pryce

Good Friday

The sun shines on the wooded hillside,
the daffodils are in full bloom;
pale lemon clumps of primroses,
lambs gambolling in the fields.
Spring is in the air —

Ubi caritas et amor,
ubi caritas Deus ibi est.

The procession moves up the hillside
following Jesus carrying the cross,
re-enacting the passion of God
in the tumult of our world.
Music is in the air —

Ubi caritas . . .

Jesus falls with the weight of the cross —
Simon helped him to carry it then;
men, women and children bear it now,
those who suffer with AIDS.
There is praise in the air —

Ubi caritas . . .

The women of Jerusalem weep —
'Do not weep for me,' he says;
'weep for yourselves and your children.'

I start to cry in the stillness.
Tears are in the air —

Ubi caritas . . .

Women have lost their children,
their men have been taken away,
those they care for have died;
they too are affected.
AIDS is in the air —

Ubi caritas . . .

The women around the world
who care as best they can,
they too are infected with AIDS;
tears are all they can give.
Sobs rend the air —

Ubi caritas . . .

Do not tell me not to weep —
my grief is too deep for words,
I remember those I have loved . . .
my friends who have died with AIDS.
Tears are a gift —

Ubi caritas . . .

Remember your children, Lord Jesus,
all those who die through AIDS;
they share with you in your passion,
be there to greet them at last.
Weep with me —

Ubi caritas . . .

Pat Wright

Pain

Pain,
Perpetual pain,
Aching, slogging, grieving,
feeling,
piercing, future blinding
round embracing,
isolating,
oneness
loneness
weary sadness making.

Pain of watching,
waiting
nothing certain
one year, two years
time is breaking over
day by day
and holding in its grasp
our lives and loss

Pain of never winning
not improving
slowly waiting
for the end that will be no end
but start again of grieving
paining,
pining
further anger
sadness

Pain of being rendered helpless.
Nothing cures
though love can ease the time
of days and nights of
help me, turn me, lift me
feed me,
touch me softly, giving
hopeful love's embrace.

Is this empty
PAIN of inner man?
Analgesics cannot touch
this deeper hurt.
Can it covered be by
alcohol's soft dream
or drugs' high lift?

Is there in the hurt
endured,
a glimpse of Christ
hanging, waiting, paining
on the tree.
Is this pain a part
of when our Lord
is crossing me?

No answer have I
Only this I say
that when I look at him
He is with me.

Ivan Mann

I cry out to the void

A version of Psalm 6

Refrain: I cry out to the Void:
How long, O God, how long?

Hideous afflictions of a turbulent age —
virus, cancer, thrombosis, ulcer —
warheads in the fluids of my being:
I am caught in a world that is twisted,
trapped in its web of corruption,
tempted to blame my ills on to 'them',
tempted to avoid the hatred within.

Hard pressed by anxiety and discord,
carriers of disease, injectors of poison,
overwhelmed by malice and fear,
paralysed, depressed, we cannot move,
spun in the vortex of death.

Distressed in the very depths of our being,
bones shaking, cell mutating,
we are almost in despair.

In your mercy and grace set us free.
Refine us in the fire of your love.
Our cry is of hope, yet struggling with doubt,
a stammer gasping for breath in the night.

Turn your face to me, save my life;
deliver me in the endurance of love,
ease the burden of guilt and of pain,
let me know the grace of your presence,
now in this life and through the shades of the grave.

I am weary with my suffering,
every night I flood my bed with tears.
I drench my couch with weeping,
my eyes waste away out of grief,
I grow weak through the weight of oppression.

You that work evil and seek to destroy,
Loosen your grip, away from my presence.
For God has heard the sound of my weeping,
forgives me with delight and lightens my gloom.
The destroyers will be ashamed and sore troubled:
trembling, they will be stripped of their power,
no longer able to harm.

And no, I will not gloat or hate,
in the Love of God I will hold on to you yet.
In the anger and hope of the wrath of our God,
come to the place of repentance and mercy.
And you, silent virus, invisible, malignant,
bound up with my bodily being,
are you an enemy that I can befriend,
or at least contain in a place of your own —
your power to harm taken away,
brought with us to the glory of God?

*God of mercy and tenderness, giver of life and conqueror of
death, look upon our weakness and pain, and bring us to health
and to wholeness, that we may sing a new song to your praise;
through Jesus Christ, Redeemer of the powers.*

Jim Cotter

PART TWO

'And who is my neighbour?'

'And who is my Neighbour?'

(Luke 10.29)

I want to share a story with you, a story from the United States. It's a very simple story about a man called Paul. At the time when it all happened, Paul was in his thirties. Some would say he was a typical middle-class American: he lived in a rich, white suburb on the outskirts of Chicago, in a big respectable suburban house. The house was enormous, beautifully decorated and furnished, with long green lawns reaching down to a tree-lined avenue. It had a wide drive and garaging for two wide American cars. The garage door opened automatically at the flick of a switch.

Paul lived there with Charles, who happened to be Paul's lover. Like Paul, Charles was a successful and rich lawyer. Together they lived a decent law-abiding life: working very hard, enjoying all the benefits of the high salaries and vibrant social lives that their professional status afforded them.

Each evening, Paul would drive home from his office in the centre of Chicago, seated in his large, plush car. He would look down sometimes through the tinted glass of the windows, down onto the houses below the fly-overs along which he sped. He would look down on the crowded streets or at the squalid backs of the tenement blocks where the poor blacks lived, and he would drive on. Paul never ventured into those areas: to be honest, for all his power and his wealth, he was a little afraid of the people that lived down there — afraid of the cultures and lifestyles below that were so different from his own. The places beneath the fly-over he associated with crime, indecency, danger.

He felt much more secure with the broad, well-lit

39

streets of the white suburbs: with his rich, respectable lawyer friends; good, wholesome Americans who earned an honest dollar — like the ones he worshipped with most Sundays at the local church. You could trust them.

One autumn Charles went down suddenly with a 'flu'-like illness which dogged him for weeks. What seemed like flu rapidly became pneumonia, and Charles was hospitalized. Soon after the doctor called Paul in and told him that Charles's immunity system had broken down — that he had AIDS.

Paul was devastated — quite naturally, his world had been turned upside down — the person he loved, with whom he shared his life, had been diagnosed as having a terminal illness. It was not that there were financial worries, both he and Charles could afford all the medical care and attention that would be necessary. It was the sudden emotional need that shocked him. He had never felt helpless before.

Paul felt sure that his church would support them both. He turned hopefully to the pastor, and dutifully the pastor came to their home. But the pastor was very afraid. Paul was not sure whether the pastor was afraid of Charles's illness, or afraid of his love for Charles. But when the pastor came he took the opportunity to give Paul and Charles a piece of his mind, and then he hurried on his way to take a service. He didn't want to come near the situation. Perhaps he wasn't able to.

Paul felt sure their friends would support him: his decent, respectable friends with whom he had always seemed to have so much in common. But when Paul telephoned to tell them the news, they suddenly fell silent, and made excuses about having to rush on to an important meeting. They never called, or visited. Sometimes Paul saw them drive past the house on their way to work. They were so busy.

Suddenly Paul and Charles were very isolated and very alone. One day, in desperation, Paul turned to an organization for people with HIV and their families. A woman called Eunice came to see them at home. She was a black lady, in her fifties. Her son Godwin had suffered with AIDS, and died.

Eunice visited Paul and Charles regularly at home, and in hospital. It was she, and only she, who stuck with Paul through the long painful months of Charles's illness; and when the time came, she did her best to help Paul face life without Charles.

And Paul never forgot her kindness and her lack of fear, nor how one night when he took Eunice home in his car, he found that Eunice lived in a tenement block down under, beneath the fly-overs.

James Woodward

Creators with God

Where would we be today, if women, men, and even children, had not come forward at times when humanity seemed to be heading for the worst? They held on to a fine hope in humanity and to an invisible presence.

They found a way to go beyond personal conflicts and to cross the barriers which separate nations and people of different spiritual families or races. They perceived, rising up from the heart of the peoples of the earth, an aspiration to a fullness of joy and peace, but also an endless lamentation.

As for you, are you going to let yourself fall asleep in dull indifference? If you are dismayed by the mistrust that exists between nations and by the wounds left by broken human relationships, will you let your lips and your heart become frozen in an attitude of: 'What's the use, we can do nothing, let things take their course.'

Are you going to let yourself sink into discouragement like Elijah, a believer of times gone by, who, seeing that he could do nothing more for his people, lay down under a tree to fall asleep and forget?

Or will you remain awake? You have a long journey ahead of you. Will you take your place among those women, men and children who have decided to act?

They possess unsuspected strengths. By their very simplicity, their lives speak to us. They foster sharing and solidarity, and dispel the paralysis of indifference. They disarm mistrust and hatred. They are bearers of trust and reconciliation. Knowing that God does not wish armed conflicts or any other human suffering, they take action.

By doing all they can to make the world a place fit to live in, by understanding with a trusting heart and living by forgiveness, they become creators with God.

If a passion to forgive became a burning flame within you, you would be kindling a spark of communion that reaches even the most tragic situations.

Do we not realize that God wants us to be creators with him. He has accepted a huge risk: he has wanted human beings not to be like passive robots, but free to decide on the direction their lives will take. He leaves us free to forgive, but free also to reject forgiveness; free to create with God or not.

The depths of the human being are limitless. They open towards the depths of God. And God is already there waiting for every person, deep within them. It is there that creative energy is born.

Brother Roger of Taizé

The point of prayer

He who prays
stands at that point
of intersection
where the love of God
and the tensions and sufferings
we inflict on each other
meet and are held
in the healing power of God.

Mother Mary Clare SLG

God's people

God calls us as a people, a whole people in whom no one is expendable. We are called to bear witness to the Good News that no one is a stranger or an outsider; that in Jesus all division and separation have been broken down. In the face of the world crisis of AIDS, we are called to be one people and yet hardness of heart, discrimination and oppression prevent us from being who God calls us to be. For this we ask forgiveness:

God of compassion, we often misrepresent you as a God of wrath, yet you are the God of love, raising us all to life; and so we ask:
Jesus, remember me, when you come into your kingdom!

Lord Jesus, you banish the fear that has paralysed us, your Church, in responding to the needs of all who are affected by HIV or AIDS. When we falter, encourage us and strengthen us; and so we ask:

Jesus, remember me . . .

Spirit of unity, you build us up when we break down; you gather in when we exclude; you affirm when we condemn; and so we ask:

Jesus, remember me . . .

May God the Creator, Redeemer and Sustainer, have mercy on us, forgive us our sin and bring us all to everlasting life. Amen.

Martin Pendergast

Open our hearts

Creator God, open our hearts and minds to see you not only in power and glory, but in weakness and rejection, so that as we pray, we may have that mind in us which was in Christ Jesus who was smitten and wounded for our sake:

We pray that in the midst of this world and before the eyes of all people with whom we are united in our common humanity, we may live the Good News of God's reign.

Lord, in your mercy
Hear our prayer

We give thanks for the Gospel of healing and liberation which is preached to the whole Church in the ministry of those with HIV or AIDS. We pray that we may be open to receive this gift.

Lord in your mercy
Hear our prayer

As we listen to the words of all who suffer, may we become more aware of their needs. May we recognize that as one part of the body is gifted with life and healing, so is the whole.

Lord in your mercy
Hear our prayer

On this World AIDS Day we remember all those in this country and across the world who suffer . . . (you may wish to add specific countries or particular development agencies). We give thanks for all who care for people living with HIV or AIDS, remembering especially the work of Body Positive, the Haemophilia Society, The Terrence Higgins Trust and many local groups, including . . . (you may wish to add local groups), and other hospices and centres of support. We pray for these and all who are involved in research and hospital care, that in their endeavours they may always respect the precious dignity of the human person.

Lord in your mercy
Hear our prayer

Martin Pendergast

A prayer for healing

Blessed are you, Lord of All, giving new life and health to those who call upon you. Usher in your kingdom and manifest your power to heal those with AIDS [and ARC].

Blessed are you, Lord of Wisdom, who pushes back the borders of darkness and disease. Enlighten those who search for a cure for AIDS [and ARC] and strengthen those who care for our suffering brothers and sisters.

Blessed are you, Lord of Love and Peace. Be with the families and loved ones of those who live with this disease. Touch us all with your love and make us instruments of your healing.

A prayer from Uganda

Keep us, Sovereign Lord from panic when crisis and panics arise. Help us to know that though you do not always remove troubles from us you always accompany us through them.

A short prayer for a big need

God help everyone living with AIDS.
Guard their lives and their loved ones.
Guide their healers and their helpers.
Give us all new wholeness and new hope.

Martin Pendergast

Our common humanity

Blessed are you, God of life, for in Jesus, the servant of all, we see your human face.

We give thanks for the good news of healing and liberation which is preached to the whole world by those who live with HIV or AIDS.

We pray that in the midst of this world, and before the eyes of all people with whom we are united through our common humanity, we may listen to their words so as to become more aware of their needs.

May we recognize that as one part of the body suffers, so also does the whole. As one part of the body is gifted with life and healing, so also is the whole. Then, may we proclaim our hope in the coming of your reign when all will be one in a new humanity, and you will be all in all, God, for ever and ever. Amen.

Martin Pendergast

Trust

Loving God, you show yourself to those who are vulnerable and make your home with the poor and weak of this world;
Warm our hearts with the fire of your Spirit. Help us to accept the challenges of AIDS.

Protect the healthy, calm the frightened, give courage to those in pain, comfort the dying and give to the dead eternal life;
Console the bereaved, strengthen those who care for the sick.

May we your people, using all our energy and imagination, and trusting in your steadfast love, be united with one another in conquering all disease and fear.

Terrence Higgins Trust Interfaith Group

In God's image

Blessed are you, our God, for in Jesus you show us the image of your glory. We give thanks for the gospel of healing and liberation which is preached to the whole Church in the ministry of those with HIV or AIDS. May we recognize that it is the real body of Christ which suffers at this time through HIV and AIDS. It is the real mind of Christ which is racked by fear and confusion. It is the real image of God in Christ which is blasphemed in prejudice, oppression and poverty. May we see in this crisis, loving God, not punishment but the place where God is most powerfully at work in Jesus Christ, and where, as sisters and brothers, we can lead each other to life in all its fullness, given in the same Christ our Lord. Amen.

Catholic AIDS Link

Guilt

A Carer's greatest fear
I have been guilty again —
Guilty of being tired
Guilty of possession
Did I do that right?
Guilty of pushing that fear down hard
Guilty of being hurt and hurting
Of making decisions
Guilty of crying

Did I try as hard as I should?
Guilty of keeping my emotions in check and not
    succeeding
Of not communicating
Guilty of exploding with my frustration
Can I do better tomorrow. Guilty
And then my absolute exhaustion makes me feel guilty,
Can't I have two more minutes to myself, on my own.
Guilty
But today I am much better, guilty of being
A good Carer
Guilty of loving and caring and knowing
I have got it right
And tomorrow I will be guilty again
Guilty of not feeling guilty
Till tomorrow I will feel alright
But then, I really must find a new guilt
I have used all these before

Ross Davis

In God's love

Divine Lover,
so fill me with yourself that I may be all love.
Transform my self-centredness
in your penetrating love and compassion.

In the power of your love dwelling in me,
may I now radiate

> Love . . .
> Compassion . . .
> Joy . . .
> Peace . . .

Within this radiation of love I place

> my family . . .
> my friends . . .
> my colleagues . . .
> those who have trusted me with their secrets . . .
> those whom I love and like . . .
> those whom I cannot yet like . . .
> those who are my enemies . . .
> those to whom are entrusted power, influence,
> decision . . .
> those in trouble . . . sorrow . . . anxiety . . .
> illness . . .
> those who are jubilant . . .
> those who are quietly contented . . .
> those who are dying . . .
> those who have died . . .
> all humankind . . .
> all creation . . .

Divine Lover,
whom the heavens adore,
may the whole earth worship you,
all tongues confess you,
all peoples obey you,
and all your friends love and serve you
in unity, trust, and peace.

Jim Cotter

Anointing

Blessing of the oil

Eternal and loving God,
bless this oil
and bless those who receive its anointing in trust,
that it may be to them
an eternal medicine,
a spiritual remedy,
an inward consecration,
to their strengthening, healing, and joy;
through Jesus Christ our Saviour.

Bidding to all

In the name of God,
who is great and good and love,
in the name of God,
giving life, bearing pain, making whole:

by this oil
may we/you be warmed and soothed:
may the healing Spirit
penetrate the cells and fibres of our/your being,
that we/you may become whole,
giving thanks to God always and in all places,
and being ready to venture further on the way of faith;

by this oil
may we/you renew the consecration of our/your life
to the truth and service of God,
being not afraid to encounter God alone,
nor of dying in order to live,
nor of bearing the burdens of others
with whom we/you have to do;

51

know this oil
as a sign of gladness and rejoicing,
of lamps lit and of feasting,
of mirth and of joy.

To each who receives anointing

N, through faith in the power and the will
of our Saviour Jesus Christ
to make you whole and holy,
to consecrate you with joy
for ever deeper service and friendship,
to give you courage
to go through the narrow gates of your journey,
I anoint you with oil
in the name of God,
who gives you life,
bears your pain,
and makes you whole.
Amen.

Jim Cotter

A litany

All: O God, today as we focus on HIV and
AIDS, we confront things we would often
prefer to avoid.

Leader: Here we are confronted with chaos.

People: Here we feel the surging Spirit of God who
shakes our foundations and hurls the
mountains into the sea;

Here we feel the God who upsets our order
and threatens our security.
Kyrie elesion (Lord, have mercy)

Leader: Here we are confronted with death.
People: Here we face the truth that we are
vulnerable, and mortal;
Here we face the fact that life is fragile, and
precious;
Here we face the challenge that we cannot
come to terms with our life until we have
first come to terms with our death.
Kyrie eleison

Leader: Here we are confronted with sexuality.
People: Here we discover that humanity and
sexuality are inseparable; and in Jesus Christ
we discover that divinity and carnality are
inseparable;
Here we discover that in Him our sexuality
is redeemed and not denied.
Kyrie eleison

Leader: Here we are confronted with judgement.
People: Here we stand before the judgement of God
that rejects our self-righteousness; that tears
away our efforts to justify ourselves;
that condemns our efforts to find acceptance
by condemning others.
Kyrie eleison

Leader: Here we are confronted with fear.
People: Here we face the fear of those who are
different from us;
Here we face the fear of chaos and death; of
sexuality and judgement.
Kyrie eleison

Leader:	Here we are confronted with Grace.
People:	Here we feel the embrace of God's Grace that accepts and affirms, that is faithful and merciful.
All:	Loving God, redeem us from captivity and turn our fears to freedom.
	Be with us today and bless us, in Jesus' name. Amen.

Lance Stone

PART THREE

'Dying and yet we live'

As servants of God we commend ourselves in every way: in great endurance, in troubles, hardships and distresses . . . in hard work, sleepless nights and hunger; in purity, understanding, patience and kindness; in the Holy Spirit and in sincere love; in truthful speech and in the power of God; with tools of righteousness in the right hand and in the left; through glory and dishonour, bad report and good report; genuine, yet regarded as imposters; known, yet regarded as unknown; dying, and yet we live on; beaten, and yet not killed; sorrowful, yet always rejoicing; poor, yet making many rich; having nothing, and yet possessing everything.

2 Corinthians 6.4–10

Life in death — death in life

To ask 'What is death?' is to ask 'What is life?' During the past five years or more I have been involved with many who are living with and dying of HIV infection. It is these people perhaps more than any others who are constantly nourishing me with the facts that we are *not* dying in death. It is they who constantly show me how to live in and through my own daily dying into a life that is worth living and loving. It seems to me personally that I cannot co-creatively be involved in another's dying until I am involved in my own daily losses, my own daily dying. This enables me to become the truth of who I am as a person.

It is difficult not to be afraid of death, but to see it as the key and the way into that which is full of potential. Our concern must be to *live*, being alive to this dimension, daring to release ourselves, and encouraging the dying person to live into the spiritual or wholeness potential of life. For me, being a spiritual person means daring to live the truth of my life to the full, thus becoming myself in order to be available to others.

The awareness of death can become one of the most creative and encouraging spurs to life. The denial of death is partially responsible for people living empty unfulfilled lives. They live as persons blinded and afraid to commit themselves to growth. But growth is evident in the lives of those who have allowed me into their space. They know, and they have become fully aware that they are on the way into a future beyond comprehension. This is the liberating act which means giving up all that is not being the truth of oneself; all that is chosen without choosing and accepted only to please someone else's needs. To lose that which is not truthful in oneself is to gain one's own real self. Then one is able honestly and unashamedly to love oneself and be loved unconditionally by others. Our growth into our own personal dying reminds us quite forcibly that one can only be fully oneself if one is no one else. Then one is released from their approval, whoever they are, and can look to oneself for evaluation of success and failure in terms of one's own honest and realistic aspirations.

Life is the school for learning how to be real in our sharing and to be more loving towards oneself, and each other. I believe we are born to be networked into the 'friendships of love' in the *now* moments of our ordinary every day living. This recognizing that love is the most positively active principle. Only through love can the many variables of human experience be viewed and weighed. It is the empathy of love which connects us to the wholeness of ourselves, the wholeness of humanity, and the wholeness of the all of all creation, visible and invisible. It enables us to know and see ourselves as part of a holographic mesh in which the parts are related to the whole and through the whole to each other by the empathic resonance of creation. It is this unconditional offering of love's friendships throughout the whole of humanity and from within the individual person which enables us to grow towards a death worth living.

To discuss death and dying of another person in these terms is difficult. The dying and the bereaved person do not need words, but the silence of empathy. They will know our concern more through our ability to hear as we listen attentively. In this way the dying and the bereaved person are able to listen to the loss which is happening for each other. In the silences shared they know that they are being embraced by the empathy of love's presence.

To be alongside with the courage of empathy is not at all easy. To ask the question 'Why?' as I do, is also to ask the question 'Why not?' To be alongside the dying and the bereaved person is to be involved in one of the most sacred activities as one watches helplessly the person changing physically almost beyond recognition, while at the same time he is growing more fully in another dimension of being fully alive to life. As I hear the pain of loss by being alongside the dying person I can also hear that it is okay to leave his body in his own timing. As lovers say good-bye they release each other through the courage and the dignity of their loving. They are liberating each other into the mystery of their respective futures.

To be given this privilege is to be given one of the most co-creative experiences. They are for me of a spiritual nature and have nothing to do with religion *per-se*, but everything with living one's life to the full. This has been confirmed not only by my own personal experiences, but

59

by those who have shared some of their experiences with me.

I would never have missed his dying for all the gifts in the world. Even though at times I could hardly hold his emaciated body; even though I could hardly contain my own pain and my own dying in his dying.

During the whole period of my friend's dying we grew closer together as lovers. We were constantly learning about each other until his last breath what it means to love and be loved.

We learned that being alongside each other in partnership was as enriching in illness as in health. We learned that being alongside each other enriched us more than all our sexual activities. Our loving expanded to include the wholeness of each other and the wholeness of his dying and my dying in his dying.

I feel I can say we became more whole, more spiritual through our body–mind contacts, as we touched each other's soul, each other's uniqueness, each other's mystery, each other's undying love. Our loving became the invisible fabric of our lives woven together upon the loom of life and death for all time.

These statements all confirmed my own thoughts and feelings which the loss of some very dear friends from HIV infection brought. Through the tears of our loss we are saying individually and collectively, 'Love is the link between life and death and between death and life.' Love is the invisible fabric of the whole of creation. I know that I will not lose the love which has been so freely gifted to me throughout my life by both men and women lovers who have made the pilgrimage into the greater mystery. They have taken with them all the love I was able to offer. I know their greatest legacy to me is the gift of their loving me, which is now a part of myself for all time and nourishing me especially during my most vulnerable times. Love says to each one of us 'I am in you and you are in me' for all time, echoing words from St John's Gospel — 'At that day ye shall know that I am in my Father, and ye in me and I in you' (John 14.20). This is a reminder to me that there can be no Kingdom of Love without Love first being in oneself. It also reminds me that 'He who is in the openness of love loves me in whatever he sees. Whatever this man may live, in truth this man lives in me' (*Bhagavad Gita* VI.30).[1]

I have seen these changes occurring in the dying and bereaved persons once they have grasped and accepted the fact that they are in the final stages of growth. I have seen how dying releases the factors that inform us that life is worth living and dying for: compassion, courage, acceptance, patience, faith, hope and love. What is important is to recognize that whether we understand fully why we are suffering, or what will happen when we die, our prime purpose as human persons is to grow into our fullest potential through our different dyings as we dare to look within ourselves to find and build the stillness of peace. It is from within this stillness that the dying and the bereaved person reach out to each other and to others with guidance of faith, the patience of hope and love's eternalizing embrace.

Dying and death are the great equalizers of persons whatever the nature of the dying or at whatever age one dies. Death reminds us more than any other thing that we are all one in death and that there are no borders to death. We are all born with the same destiny to love and to die.

The dying and the bereaved demand that we see the

person behind the label as they need the same loving and caring as we do. This comes about as we recognize and accept each other's courage, and each other's value systems and honour each other's humanity by recognizing the fact we all have an inner knowledge of our needs. Making promises that can be realistically fulfilled is necessary, but essential is the promise of truth.

Every dying is unique because no person has died before. In his dying he wants honesty and a presence that is comfortable and comforting of the kind that dignifies his dying.

Those of us involved in being alongside the dying and the significant other person in his or her life, will occasionally be aware of the fact that some wish to select the mode and the time of their dying, especially when this dying person feels from within his or her inmost being that life no longer has any meaning or quality. If this person has not already done so, he will arrange for some assistance which he knows to be outside the doctor's or nurse's treatment and care. Yet helping people to die is not a new phenomenon. It has gone on throughout the history of humankind.

I am aware that some lovers may very well have acceded to their dying lover's wish to be released from this life. They are usually partners who love each other very much. I have respected their maturity, their integrity of purpose at being able to arrive at this decision, when on the whole society's attitude is against any form of death other than what is deemed natural.

Suicide is not the right term which fits what has been planned. Euthanasia is not a suitable word either, for it tends to imply the mercy of one person to another. Self-selected death is a more realistic term. The whole idea of terminating one's life has been thought through long before the event. It is well planned in advance and deals with the notion of death itself as not being the end, but rather the fulfillment of life.

Dying is a mystery; it has been called, 'the final stage of growth'.[2] It is a mystery beyond all understanding. There is no doubt in my mind that life is for dying and dying is for living our fullest potential. Only through a recognition and acceptance of my own vulnerability to death will I become my own real self, my own full potential, seeded with my own personal uniqueness. There is no doubt that only by being fully alive are we able to live into our dying. Life and death spiral into each other and into the wholeness of creation which is constantly re-creating its co-creativeness. I have seen this happen so often during the past few years.

It is the gift of personal love offered and received that enables us to realize and accept that in death nothing is wasted. All is caught up in the co-creativeness of love's endeavouring, reminding us that death belongs to life, as birth does in initiating us into living this life. It is through being alongside so many that I am convinced we move on into the next life within a 'Cloud of Unknowing'. Elizabeth Kubler-Ross reminds us: 'There is no total death. Only the body dies. The seed or spirit or whatever you may wish to label it, is eternal. You may interpret this in any way that makes you comfortable.'[3]

For me the death of each person signifies that his or her work of loving is finished in this dimension of being. Edith Sitwell wrote: 'Love is not changed by death and nothing is lost and all in the end is harvest.' And T. S. Eliot wrote: 'In my end is my beginning.' These are reminders that life is full of endings and beginnings.

It seems to me that the completeness of life is the death of life as we know it. It is the total release of the person into the life of love's unending mystery. This fact becomes a reality as we learn to look at the life that so enriched us, instead of this death and this departing, and try to accept and recognize that in love there is no departing. Death in life leads to life in death.

Bill Kirkpatrick

References
1. D. Lorimer, *Whole in One* (Akana 1990).
2. Dr E. Kubler-Ross, *Death — The final stage of growth*, New York, Simon & Schuster, 1986.
3. Kubler-Ross, *Death*.

Do not be afraid

We have got to live now in and through the dying, in order that we may bear witness to the resurrection life . . . If we live in this glorious perspective, we do not have to wait for the fullness of life after death. Life in God is here and now, experienced first and foremost by experiencing death. Do not be afraid to die, do not be afraid when you are overwhelmed by the sense of your own weakness and sin and muck and desolation. Let everything which is in you, and everything which is thrown up against you by the power of evil, be held in Christ's healing power. Do not absorb it or be overcome by it, but let it in you meet Christ's power to heal; let it in you meet this almighty power of God, so that in you the mess can be transformed, answered.

Mother Mary Clare SLG

Acceptance

Acceptance does not mean suffering. Suffering puts walls around pain, closes in on it, and tries to change it. Acceptance allows pain to move. Suffering, like self-pity, holds on to disturbing thoughts and keeps them hostage. Acceptance lets them pass.

Suffering despairs and curses fate behind God's back. Acceptance stands at the top of the hill, faces the wind, throws back his shoulders and screams. Acceptance allows energy to move.

Accepting 'that person, place, or thing' doesn't mean we have to like it. We don't have to like our illnesses or situations. We don't have to be quiet about them either. It's okay to make a fuss, even a big fuss. Acceptance means letting energy move. It means we're alive.

Anon

The teacher within

The teacher is within, so you have to learn to be still . . . you have to learn to live your life so that you are listening within, no matter what you are doing.
Bartholomew

To become acquainted with the teacher within, we need to spend time alone. We need to give our inner teacher the time and space to make his or her presence known to us.

We may also need help from other people. They can help us learn how to meditate, how to listen and we can join with other people and our mutual seeking can help us find what we're looking for.

Each of us can find the outside support we need, even if we have to get it over the telephone or through the mail.

Making the change from running through life with our spiritual ears plugged to listening requires only a little willingness and a little practice. Our teachers are waiting to help us.

Anon

Reaching out

(For the service for World AIDS Day, Westminster Abbey, November 1990)

Wrapped in the bloody rags of her shame, exhausted by washing and changing, embarrassed by the knowledge that all her neighbours knew, the woman with the issue of blood waited for her chance.

Each time she went down to the washing place she could see the gossips eyeing her with a delicate and half-discreet curiosity. If she could have afforded to she would have buried evening by evening, each soiled cloth, but unmarriageable, untouchable, always in a state of un-cleanliness that would curse even the food she cooked, she had no access to money. And no one ever touches her.

Once in four weeks other women would join her, one by one. They were frightened of her; she exposed the fragility of their safety. They would hush their voices, kind but cruel. And no one ever touches her.

Twelve years. Four thousand, three hundred and eighty

days. And what had she ever done to earn such a fate? At what secret moment had she offended what unknown code? She examined her conscience, but there was nothing — she was innocent, she had been not one jot more sinful than any other woman in the village. And as she walked through the days she could feel her rage growing heavy inside her; bitterness flowed in to fill the spaces where her blood flowed out. And no one ever touches her.

But still there was in her a fierceness; she held her head high. she would not bow to their definitions. They called it pride, she called it dignity. All she knew was that she needed her fierceness more than she needed their definitions.

So when she hears about the Teacher, the man who embraces lepers and loves prostitutes, she knows what she has to do. There is fear and shame, but she knows what she has to do, and she believes that she can do it. And hope has two lovely daughters, courage and anger. She needs them both; she has lived too long alone and she is frightened in the crowd. She knows they will be angry if they see her there, and she needs her own anger to keep pushing against them. She knows her shame, and she needs her courage to fight it. She holds her fierce and thorny flower of hope, redder than any blood.

She hears that he touches people and they are healed. But she cannot do it that way. She cannot beg or accept any longer. She will do the touching this time. But at the moment when she reaches out her hand something changes, because he is different from other men. He is yearning and tender. He is not afraid of his own needs. He does not project them on to her. She is not a victim, but someone who can give him something. When she touches him the bleeding ceases and she knows in her body that she is healed.

He does not heal her; he lets her heal herself. He does not give her hope; he lets her own hope bring her to the place of exchange, to the place of love. They touch each other, because she has hope and courage and anger and he has generosity and humility and self-knowledge.

When she reaches out and touches his long cloak the bleeding stops.

Sara Maitland

Suffering and hope

To endure loss, to grieve, to feel hopeless, in short to suffer, seems inevitable. Suffering is inextricably linked to living and at some time, in different ways, we all suffer. It is something subjective and comparisons are unhelpful, to be told 'it could be worse' is not often a consolation when we feel pain.

However, it seems to me that suffering is at its most terrible, when it appears to be without either good cause or good reason. Sometimes past I have suffered as a result of my own folly or stupidity. In retrospect I have been able to see how suffering has led me to grow, become more whole, to change for the better. (Changing, after all, is almost always a painful process.) Therefore it has seemed to be, in one way or another, justified. However, to suffer and endure that darkness wherein one can see no logic, no rhyme nor reason to it, this is most painful of all. It is terrible, frustrating, frightening and challenging. All at the same time.

For me it means the removal (however temporary) of any sense of hope. With hope, all manner of things can be endured. As they say 'a light at the end of the tunnel' will spur us on. Without a sense of hope however, the temptation to give in, to give up, is great indeed.

Christ too must have experienced this sense of isolation, this hopelessness. He too descended into the darkness where there seems to be no reason, no good. Perhaps in the garden of Gethsemane, or in that moment when he cried out 'My God, my God, why have you forsaken me?' For Christ too, suffering was an inevitable part of living.

I do not mean to suggest that suffering is in itself good. Nor that it is a state of being to which we should become accustomed. We should not be complacent, resigning ourselves to suffer in this 'vale of tears', offering up our pain for the 'poor souls'. We are called after all, to be a people of joy. God's will is for us to be whole, holy, happy.

However, when we are in that dark place where we can see no light at all, we can remind ourselves that after the crucifixion, after the passion and death, there was the resurrection. In Christ we have reason for hope. Sustained by faith, we can see in him the perfect example of one who suffered, sometimes doubted, but in the end triumphed.

So for myself too, I will embrace the suffering and look forward to the resurrection.

A person living with HIV

A litany of reconciliation

Almighty God, creator of life, sustainer of every good thing I know, my partner with me in the pain of this earth, hear my prayer as I am in the midst of separation and alienation from everything I know to be supportive, and healing, and true.

AIDS has caused me to feel separated from you. I say, 'Why me, what did I do to deserve this?' . . . Help me to remember that you do not punish your creation by bringing disease, but that you are Emmanuel, God with us. You are as close to me as my next breath.

AIDS has caused a separation between the body I knew and my body now . . . Help me to remember that I am more than my body and, while it pains me greatly to see what has happened to it, I am more than my body . . . I am part of you and you me.

AIDS has separated me from my family . . . Oh God help me and them to realize that I haven't changed, I'm still their child, our love for each other is your love for us . . . Help them overcome their fear, embarrassment and guilt . . . Their love brought me into this world . . . Help them share as much as possible with me.

AIDS has caused a separation between me and my friends; my friendships have been so important to me. They are especially important now . . . Help me O God to recognize their fear, and help them to realize my increasing need for them to love in any way they can.

AIDS has separated me from my society, my work world and my community . . . It pains me for them to see me differently now . . . Forgive them for allowing their ignorance of this disease and their fear to blind their judgements . . . Help me with my anger towards them.

AIDS has caused a separation between me and my Church . . . Help the Church restore its ministry to 'the least of these' by reaching out to me and others . . . Help them suspend their judgements and love me as they have before . . . Help me and them to realize that the Church is the Body of Christ . . . that separation and alienation wound the body.

God of my birth and God of my death, help me know you
have been, you are, and you are to come . . . Amen.

Anon

A healthy person

The whole of me, the whole person,
physical, mental, emotional, spiritual,
is in need of being healed,
of being made whole.
The curing of physical symptoms
is but one part of this process:
the absence of cure need not hinder it.

Illness is not an unfortunate incident,
but a phase of life with its own time and meaning.

The words 'healing' and 'salvation' are close:
they derive from the same Greek root, 'sozein'.
We experience moments of salvation,
the gift and the grace of freedom,
of breathing again in wide open spaces,
of being sprung from the trap,
released from confinement or oppression.

My own healing is bound up with that of others.
I need to pray and work
for the healing of the nations,
for food for the hungry,
for justice for the downtrodden,
for my neighbours in a global village.
Without their well-being
I cannot be completely well.

Everything that I am and do
contributes to the making of my soul-body,
and the making of the soul-bodies of others,
and the coming to glory of the whole universe.
The eye of faith looks to a transfiguration
of everything that is of agony or ecstasy
in the life of my flesh-body,
of the flesh-bodies of others,
of the material stuff of this earth and beyond.

Through grace and in faith
I receive the gift of eternal life,
abiding close to the self-giving love of God,
the love that is not destroyed by death.

Jim Cotter

A form of the Eucharist

President: We are here together in the name of Jesus
healer, teacher and way of salvation

All: We are sisters and brothers to him
daughters and sons of the Living God
Alleluia Alleluia

Opening prayer

Living God, source of light and life
we come to you as broken members of your
body
your strength is our strength
your health is our health
and your being, our being.

Grant us your healing in our lives
your love in our pain
and your peace in our hearts

Through Jesus Christ, your Son and our
Lord
Amen.

Act of penitence

President: All have sinned and come short of the glory
of God

All: Forgive us, O God

President: For the wounds we inflict on our sisters and
brothers

All: Forgive us O God

President: For the wounds we inflict on your creation

All: Forgive us O God

President: For the wounds we inflict on ourselves

All: Forgive us O God

President: Give your healing O God that we might
learn to forgive others as you forgive us

All: (*Turning to one another and making the sign of
the cross*)
God forgives you
Forgive others
Forgive yourself

Gloria

Glory be to God in heaven
and peace to all people on earth
Merciful God, giver of life
we worship you and give you thanks
and we praise your glorious name.

Jesus Christ, gift of God,

you cleanse us from our sins.

Show us your mercy and receive our
prayers.

For you reign with God in heaven
With the Holy Spirit you rule
to the glory of all creation.

Amen.

First reading

Psalm

Gospel

Intercessions

The peace

President: May the peace of God
the peace of the Son
and the peace of the Holy Spirit
be with you and those whose lives touch
yours.

All: Amen.

The sign of peace is exchanged

Preparation of the gifts

President: Jesus said, Where two or three are gathered
in my name there am I.

All: Come Jesus Christ and make yourself
known to us in the breaking of the bread
and the sharing of the cup.

Eucharistic prayer

President: The Lord is with us

All: Alleluia

President:	Raise your hearts and minds to God
All:	Alleluia
President:	Give thanks and praise the Holy Name
All:	Alleluia Alleluia
President:	Blessed are you Lord God healer of the sick and wounded and source of our salvation.

You have made us one and in your image
In giving us your Son you have redeemed us
and revealed to us your glory
The whole creation echoes with your praise.

Through his work on earth and life
among us
your Son showed us the depth of your love
freed us from unending death and gave us
life eternal.

Therefore we join the hosts of heaven
in their unceasing song of glory.

All: Holy! Holy! Holy!
God of all creation
The earth and the heavens glorify your
name.

President: How glorious is your creation O God
and worthy of our praise.
To you be glory and majesty forever.
You created us in your own likeness
and make us whole in you.
As a sign of your love you gave us your Son
to live on earth and suffer for our sins.

In human form and body
he loves us as his own and showed us the
power of love.

75

Divested of all worldly power,
weak and yet still strong,
child and yet still man,
wounded and yet still healed,
he gave us hope and bought us our salvation
by dying on the cross and rising to new life.
He overcame the darkness of sin and death
and offered us new life in him.

And now by the power of the Spirit who was
his healing gift
let this bread and wine become his body and
blood.

On his last night among us, he was at table
with his friends.

Stripped of his garments and wrapped only
in a towel he washed the feet of all those
present.
Taking bread during supper, he broke it and
shared it with his friends. He said,

**This bread is for you, it is my body which
I freely give you
Do this to remember me.**

After the meal was over he shared with them
the cup. He said,

**This cup is for you, it is my blood.
It will be spilt for you and for the
forgiveness of all sin.
Do this to remember me.**

All: God is with us
God is one of us
God will remain with us

President: Gathered together we now celebrate our life in you.
As we recall the sacrifice of your Son and offer our memorial to you we remember all who suffer.
We pray for all those among us living with HIV and AIDS.
On our journey together with you we seek the healing touch of your hand, so that we may be one with each other and filled with the joy of loving you.
We thank you for the gift of life in your Spirit and nourished by your body and blood may we become one body and one spirit.

We pray for your pilgrim Church,
that she may know the truth of your love and reveal your glory to all people.
We pray for all who work in your church that, guided by the love of your Son they may seek to bring the power of that love to all whom they touch.
Listen we pray to all our supplications that in you our lives may reflect the promises of eternity with you
We remember before you all who have died that they may enjoy eternal life with Christ.

All: Through him, with him and in him
In the unity of the Holy Spirit
All honour and glory are yours O God
from all who stand before you
now and forever. Amen.

The Lord's Prayer
Communion
Silence
Closing prayer
Dismissal

Sebastian Sandys
Kate Gibbs

PART FOUR

'Love is strong as death'

Set me as a seal upon your heart,
 as a seal upon your arm;
for love is strong as death,
 jealousy is cruel as the grave.
Its flashes are flashes of fire,
 a most vehement flame.
Many waters cannot quench love,
 neither can floods drown it.
If a man offered for love
 all the wealth of his house,
 it would be utterly scorned.

Song of Solomon 8.6–7 (RSV)

Letting go in sex and in death

Because of the letting go of self
that can occur at the height of orgasm,
there is a hint of death in sexual intercourse.
Because of a new sexually transmittable virus,
with the potential for disfigurement and death,
that hint is now shouting.
Physically and psychologically,
AIDS is omnipresent where sex is concerned.
It nudges us to come to terms with death.
It reminds us that there are limits
to the satisfactions of making love sexually.

Within it there always seems to be the desire for
   more —
in terms both of repetition
and of deeper and more lasting union.
Sex never yields all that it promises.
The challenge is to be glad for what it does yield
and also to acknowledge its limitations,
and so to live in the tension,
accepting that all our unions are transient.

> And the opportunity is given us to get to know
> 'the root and depth in thee
> from whence all thy faculties come forth
> as lines from a centre,
> or as branches from the body of a tree.
> This depth is called the centre, the fund,
> or bottom of the soul.'

'Such is the deep Christ-Self at the core of us,
the realm of abundant life,
the indestructible deep centre that never gives way,
the small seed which will become the great tree,
the leaven transforming the lump, the eye of the soul,
the ground of being, the heart, the transcendent self,
the extreme point at which God touches us.'

Jim Cotter

Letting go

I hope you had a restful night's sleep. Sleep is an amazing
thing isn't it? For seven or eight hours we are prepared to
let go; to surrender all control over our mind and sink into

a dream-filled darkness. When awake most of us are so anxious to keep everything under control. Yet, come the night, and we give ourselves up to the unknown. Some people find this threatening and difficult. I once went to see an extraordinary play by Samuel Beckett called *Not I*. It only lasted for twenty minutes but it was so intense you couldn't have taken more. The stage was dark except for a pair of large lips covered in phosphorescent paint. Out of this mouth came a non-stop stream of frenzied speech. It filled the theatre and became literally unbearable. This stream of terrified talk came from the mind of a person becoming unconscious, either through drugs or because they were dying. As it went under the mind sensed dark figures gathering and became terrified.

We all have something of this fear — and not only about sleep or death. T. S. Eliot has some lines in which he says, 'Do not let me hear of the wisdom of old men, but rather of . . . their fear of possession, of belonging to another, or to others or to God.' We fear to belong to others because any relationship that is worth while is not completely under our control. It involves a kind of surrender, and we would rather keep buttoned up, ourselves to ourselves. We don't want to let ourselves in for anything we can't control even when people are kind. In a play about the last war, a man in hospital was slowly dying through kidney trouble. The rest of the ward knew this and wanted to surround and support him with love. But the dying soldier couldn't receive their kindness. Even when they offered him cigarettes he refused them with the words, 'I have my own'.

And if we fear to belong to others how much more do we fear to belong to God. In his autobiography Graham Greene described how, although he had no religious belief, he wanted to marry a Catholic girl. To please her he took a course of instruction to find out what it was all about, though he had no intention of becoming a believer or of being received into the Church. The person who instructed him had once been an actor in the West End, but God had called him to the priesthood. When Graham Greene heard about this he wrote that his story 'came like a warning hand placed on my shoulder. "See the danger of going too far." That was the menace it contained. Be very careful. Keep well within your depth. There are dangerous currents out at sea which could sweep you anywhere.' Yet, against his natural inclination, he came to believe. But he described his emotions as he walked away from the baptism in these words: 'There was no joy in it at all, only a sombre apprehension. I had made the first move with a view to my future marriage, but now the land had given way under my feet and I was afraid where the tide would take me. Even my marriage seemed uncertain to me now. Suppose I discovered in myself what Father Trollope had once discovered, the desire to be a priest.'

If we want a reposeful sleep, if we want to die with peace of mind, if we want any rich relationships, if we want to believe in God, a kind of surrender is necessary — a letting go, a being prepared to be taken by the tide to where we do not know. The Christian faith says simply, 'Do not be afraid'. We let go into faithful hands. As a phrase in the Bible puts it, 'underneath are the everlasting arms'. When Christ died on the cross, according to Luke the last words he said were, 'Father into thy hands I commit my spirit'. This is the way to close our eyes in sleep or death. This is the way to face a difficult situation during the coming day. This is the way to begin the day itself.

Richard Harries

Autumn leaves

I've conducted so many services, I feel prayed out. So I sit at the back of a synagogue behind a pillar, attending not to the words but to the tunes and what they're trying to tell me.

Fortunately each Jewish festival has its signature tune. At Passover the psalms are sung to a jaunty number. At the harvest festival, they are sung to a sadder melody. A rabbi told me you can hear in it the sound of falling autumn leaves and its message to me is about letting go.

I admire people like my grandpa who can let go things. He made three fortunes, lost them, drank a whisky and held no regrets. But he pitied a textile manufacturer who jumped off the fortieth floor of a skyscraper in the 1929 slump. Hurtling past his rival's floor, the manufacturer shouted 'In-built bras with frilly trim for summer fashions'. Even at death, you see, he couldn't let go.

It's more difficult letting go people than things. A woman is waiting now by the phone, for a call that won't come. Actually she's better off without him, and one day she won't even remember his name. She just can't let go, but until she does, no one can replace him.

Life like nature abhors a vacuum and, looking back on my own life, something's always come along to fill it, though I usually didn't recognize it, because it wasn't what I expected or what I thought I wanted.

After handing in my driving licence, I had to travel on late night trains. But, amid the litter, I made unexpected friends.

When terminal patients let go life, they often let go their painkillers as well.

Now the political parties tell you how to get your rightful share of life's goodies. But religion tells you how to let it go without fuss and, facing a possible petrol shortage and recession, that's practical not pious advice.

Getting and letting go are two sides of life's coin, and you need both for happiness. That's the message of those falling leaves and what that tune is telling me.

Lionel Blue

Love will transform us

There's a saying 'pray as you can — not as you can't.' I have always understood this to mean that we should not force ourselves into a pattern or form of prayer which has no meaning for us. But what happens when we feel totally unable to pray in any shape or form? That is often my experience and I gather that I am not alone in this.

From the many occasions in my life when I have been unable to pray, one stands out particularly clearly: April 1st 1989. The scene is fresh in my mind. George, aged 34 years, was dying. His parents and Jim, his partner, were with him. It was 6 p.m. George was semi-conscious: his breathing was laboured, interrupted by bouts of coughing. On one level, it was a shocking scene: the horror and power of death, the destructiveness of the AIDS virus and our sense of helplessness in the face of such forces. But on the other hand, there were other forces at work. Wendy, George's mother, and Jim tried to raise him to ease his breathing. They sat on either side of him, their hands clasped behind his pillow, thus supporting one another to support George. His father, Ron, sat by his feet, stroking him gently, weeping.

Love one another as I have loved you, that you also should love one another. (John 13.34)

It is only in retrospect that these words are taking on a reality which is unfolding slowly. At the time, all feeling seemed to be suspended for me and words — silent or expressed — were unavailable. But there was no doubt that there was love in that room; it centred on and flowed from George. It was expressed beyond words in the linked hands which supported him. Up to that point in time it had not been easy for Wendy and Jim to accept each other and to allow their love to be shared without the competitiveness and possessiveness which often holds us captive. There is within each of us a deep longing to love and be loved, to be accepted in our uniqueness, in our vulnerable and broken selves. We experience the tension between our longing for infinite love and the limitations of our finite beings. Wendy and Jim bridged that gap when their hands joined in their love for George. The barriers we build to maintain our independence, as well as our need to be in control, the power struggles to possess love and be needed by the person we love, were demolished by their recognition that they needed one another. Love is a compelling motive. AIDS teaches us that we need each other. 'It has taken this to bring us together', is how a 21-year-old expressed it shortly before he died. No one person alone can meet the needs of another, but together we can learn to touch and allow ourselves to be touched by love. Christ demonstrated his need for support: 'stay with me' was his request to his friends when he wrestled with his fears which were so terrifying for him in Gethsemane, where he faced the imminence of death, not as a victim or sufferer, but as one who embraced death so that Love could triumph. Being with George and those who were supporting him, there was an awareness deep within me that we too were part of the Gethsemane/Calvary experience. Christ was vulnerable and needed to be supported by his friends. In the event, they 'failed' him, overwhelmed by their fatigue and their inability to be in tune with Love's request. We are so often in that position, but it is part of the wonder of Love that we are given opportunities to meet the 'God of second chances' — or the seventy-times-seven chances — who enables us to clasp hands and to reach out to each other in a variety of ways. In the diminishing moments of his life, George enabled love to take root in Wendy and Jim and allowed himself to be loved by them and by his father. Enfolded in love, it was possible to withstand the paralysing fear and power of death. It was a lesson I needed to learn, not from a position of strength — or the comfort of prayer — but by 'being there', powerless and sharing the helplessness which we all felt and allowing God to touch us in the mystery of his redemptive love.

Love works in a silent and mysterious way. There is an ongoing process of growth and much of it is in darkness, like the growth of plants and trees. Whilst we are in that darkness, we cannot see or make sense of that experience, but when we look back we can often say 'now I can see . . .' That is my experience at present, as I recall Ron's position at the foot of the bed, stroking George's feet. Some weeks earlier, George had called him during the night to sit with him because he was in pain. It was a profoundly meaningful experience for Ron. In the silence and privacy of that night there was a mutual affirmation of what it means to be father and son. In our society, with its stereotyped rules and regulations, it is not acceptable for men to express their innermost feelings openly — e.g. to caress or shed tears. To some extent that is true of all of us and when I find myself living more in my head than in my heart, prayer becomes sterile because it is devoid of the real expressions of our human existence with its mixture of intensity of conflicting feelings.

When Ron recalled the experience of that night, he remembered how George and he could cry together and that he was able to stroke his son, to comfort and reassure him and in doing so, felt reassured himself and affirmed as a father. George told me the following morning, that he had chosen to call his father rather than his mother who usually sat with him when he was in pain, because 'I did not want my dad to feel left out.' George's sensitive awareness of his father's needs, led him to reach out from his own weakness to enable strength to be built up in his father. There are strong echoes in this of Christ's words on Calvary to his mother and to John, his 'special' friend (John 19.26–7).

It is a common experience of those who are 'carers' to see in people with AIDS a depth of concern and creative sensitivity towards those who care for them. This is prayer in action and often offered by those who have been rejected by the institutional church. As a gay man, that had been George's experience. It led him to sever links with Christian organizations, calling himself an atheist. He explained to me once that he took that stance to identify with others who were marginalized as he was. Working with people who have AIDS and with their families and lovers brings us face to face with the 'God of surprises', who also experienced rejection and identified with the marginalized. I am learning that my inability to pray can stem from a lack of honesty in owning the anger I often feel with the hypocrisy of some members of the institutional church — and anger with myself at my own hypocrisy. Christ did not condemn human failure, but he was unequivocal in His condemnation of hypocrisy, especially in regard to some of the religious leaders of his time. If my prayer is going to be meaningful, I need to own and acknowledge the pain I experience in being rejected and the selectiveness of my loving which makes me reject others.

It is my belief that the experience of compassionate sharing in his pain which George offered his father, enabled him to sit at George's feet during the last few hours of his life. It enabled him also to shed tears of love, regret and anger. Ron described himself as a 'lapsed' Catholic — a term which says more about a church who rejects him because he fails to keep the letter of the law, than about Ron or his relationship with God who longs for the Spirit of the law of love to be manifested in our loving of one another as he loved us, unconditionally and with deep compassion for our own and other people's frailties and imperfections.

George died peacefully three hours after he had entered the final stages of his life's journey. He had been a care-taker in a large block of flats. The letters and floral tributes — simple bunches of flowers from the local shops and market — which were left at his door were signs of love and appreciation of George's caring for others. He was always 'there' when needed and his quality of caring went far beyond his job description. It makes me wonder if my prayer life could ever be described as going beyond my 'job description' as a Christian and a member of a religious congregation. George and others with HIV/AIDS pro-vide a new challenge to living and loving authentically in solidarity with one another in our common brokenness and also in our hope that love triumphs over death. For me the barrenness of my spiritual life is beginning to be irrigated by a growing awareness that love is a risky, exciting business, offering us constant opportunities to change and grow towards wholeness. There are times when that brings me into confrontation with God himself but, like Jacob who wrestled with God, I too would rather do that than sink into complacent security, which hides behind pious words like the bidding prayer I heard at a Catholic church on World AIDS Day: 'Let us pray for those who are suffering with AIDS, that they may be given patience and endurance'! I have no regret in saying that I ceased to 'pray' for the rest of that eucharistic celebration though at a later time it occurred to me that the appropriate response might have been Christ's prayer: 'Father forgive them, for they know not what they do.' And a little later still: 'Father forgive me, for I know not what I do'!

On the morning following George's death, Ron said to me: 'You may think this silly, but last night, when I looked at our George, I looked at Christ.' I shared with him my feeling that we were part of the Calvary experience. Reflecting on this, I wonder if we have to allow ourselves to feel the depth of our own inner emptiness, in order to allow Christ to enter and draw us into his fullness of unconditional love, so that we may share this with each other. In his last talk with his friends, George promised the gift of the Spirit, 'to guide you (us) into all truth' (John 16.13) – the truth and power of Love which sets us free.

Occasionally, I have a phone call from Ron, where he says: 'I have been talking to You-Know-Who. . . . ' Ron has a prayer corner in his sitting room where he prays as he can and it feels very good to have the invitation to share in that.

Finally, by way of epilogue or postscript, I recall the gathering of friends and relatives who crowded into George's room after the celebration of his life at his cremation. It might be difficult to stretch one's imagination to see this as a 'prayer group', yet what is prayer but the raising of heart and mind to God and expressing joy and thanks for the gift of one of his unique creations – George! What is prayer, if it is not reaching out to one another in love? This was highlighted by Ron's comment to his mother-in-law, aged 80 years, when he asked her 'I bet you never thought that you'd be in a room full of gays?' To which she replied, 'And know that there is so much love'. That response points towards a faith in a love that triumphs over death. Such faith provides the ground for hope that Love will transform us. Living with that hope, is in itself a prayer.

Eva Heyman

A peaceful death

After three days of struggle mother was exhausted. She no longer had the energy to fling her arms about in anxious movements; she could no longer even mumble prayers or cry out to God in audible words. The doctor who had seen her long, painful struggle said, 'For her it has been like running up and down a long staircase for three days. Now there is no strength left.'

We sat by her bedside, watching her breathing becoming shorter and shorter every hour. For three days we had been struggling with her, holding on to her from both sides of the bed, speaking words of comfort, praying quietly or out loud. In the past week there had been moments when we thought about the possibility of survival, brief fantasies that mother might somehow come back home and once again be with us. But, above all, there was the desire to see her open her eyes, smile, and say a few words.

The hope for a single moment of recognition, or perhaps just a few words, held us all in its grip. We kept asking ourselves and each other: 'Can she hear? Does she know that we are all with her? Does she feel our love and concern? Can she understand anything we are saying? Does she sense that we are praying for her?'

Sometimes there seemed to be a small sign of recognition, a glimmer of understanding. But mostly her eyes remained without expression and her hands no longer responded to our touch. Father looked at her and then said softly, 'I know there are so many things you would like to say, but you cannot — it's all right, we are with you.' While he was speaking these words, I felt our immense desire for a response, just a little response, a word, a nod, a smile, a movement of the hand. It seemed that we were begging for more contact.

How great is the human desire for contact! After thirty, forty or fifty years of living together, with its innumerable conversations, discussions and hours of intimate exchanges, we still wanted another sign. We were still hoping that maybe mother would bless us one more time. At times I felt guilty for desiring yet another gift from her who had given us so much. I even felt selfish and greedy. But the desire was there, strong and powerful, and we had slowly to accept that she had given us enough, more than enough.

As the hours passed it became clear that she was dying, that we would never again receive another word or gesture from her. Although we had known for the past three days that she was dying, now the awareness of finality began to touch us. There would be no new chances for expressions of thanks or regret, joy or sadness. There would be no opportunities to change anything. Never. Her life was coming to an end and our relationship with her was moving into the realm of memory. We realized that the way in which we had been her husband, son or daughter was now defined forever. The question was no longer, 'How are we going to interact with her?' but, 'How are we going to remember her?'

As we looked at her — totally exhausted from the struggle, breathing short breaths — we found our memories beginning to summarize all that had been. My father looked at me and said very quietly, 'I see my whole life with your mother passing in front of my eyes: the first time we met, our first happy days, our first little disagreements and conflicts, our hard days of working together, your birth and all that followed until now. . . . It just stands in front of my eyes like a small picture I can look at.' Looking at him, I sensed the brevity of life in my bones: a flash, a moment, a breath . . . arrival and departure . . . yesterday and today . . . all compressed in one blink of an eye. There was immense tenderness in that moment, an intimacy that I had not known before. It was not a case of the wise speaking to the unwise, the old to the young, the experienced to the inexperienced. There were no longer wise and unwise, old and young, experts and untrained. Here in the presence of death, we were indeed the same, feeling our equality as a grace.

The end came very quietly. I had left the room to make a phone call while my youngest brother and my sister were walking in the hospital corridor, talking a little between the times they spent at mother's bedside. My father and younger brother sat on either side of mother's bed, following her breathing. It had become very quiet. The nurses had just rearranged the bed, washed mother's hands and face, and combed her hair. All had become very quiet.

It was six o'clock in the evening. Father looked at her with full attention, expecting that she might still live for many hours. But then he noticed a definite slowing down of her breathing, saw her neck muscle make two more movements, and realized that she had stopped breathing. Everything was still, very still. Father bent his head, kissed her hand and cried. Then he said to my brother, 'She has died; call your brothers and sister.' As we stood around her

bed we prayed the same prayers we had said so often
during the past days. But now I added for the first time the
words we would say in the long days to come: 'May eternal
light enlighten her that she may rest in peace.'

She had simply stopped breathing. That was all. With
carefully chosen words, father told us about the final
seconds of her life, how the end had come with a slight
quiver of her neck. 'It was hardly noticeable', he said, with
a soft smile in his eyes. It had been so undramatic, so quiet.
It had hardly been an event. For a moment I felt sad
because I had not been in the room. But then I realized
that I should be grateful that father and mother had been
so close in those last moments. I recognized that it was a
gift that he, and not I, could tell the story.

Henri Nouwen

Grief

Grief cannot be shared, for it is mine alone.
Grief is a dying within me,
a great emptiness,
a frightening void.
It is loneliness,
a sickening sorrow at night,
on awakening a terrible dread.
Another's words do not help.
A reasoned argument explains little
for having tried too much.
Silence is the best response to another's grief.
Not the silence that is a pause in speech,
awkward and unwanted,
but one that unites heart to heart.

Love, speaking in silence, is the way into
the void of another's grief.
The best of all loves comes silently,
and slowly too, to soften the pain of grief,
and begin to dispel the sadness.
It is the love of God, warm and true,
which will touch the grieving heart and heal it.

He looks at the grieving person and has pity,
for grief is a great pain.
He came among us to learn about grief,
and much else too, this Man of Sorrows.
He knows. He understands.
Grief will yield to peace — in time.

Cardinal Basil Hume OSB

Death of a Son

Something has ceased to come along with me.
Something like a person: something very like one.
    And there was no nobility in it
        Or anything like that.

Something was there like a one year
Old house, dumb as stone. While the near buildings
    Sang like birds and laughed
        Understanding the pact

They were to have with silence. But he
Neither sang nor laughed. He did not bless silence
    Like bread, with words.
        He did not forsake silence.

But rather, like a house in mourning
Kept the eye turned in to watch the silence while
    The other houses like birds
        Sang around him.

And the breathing silence neither
Moved nor was still.

    I have seen stones: I have seen brick
But this house was made up of neither bricks nor stone
    But a house of flesh and blood
        With flesh of stone

    And bricks for blood. A house
Of stones and blood in breathing silence with the other
    Birds singing crazy on its chimneys.
        But this was silence,

    This was something else, this was
Hearing and speaking though he was a house drawn
    Into silence, this was
        Something religious in his silence,

    Something shining in his quiet,
This was different this was altogether something else:
    Though he never spoke, this
        Was something to do with death.

    And then slowly the eye stopped looking
Inward. The silence rose and became still.
The look turned to the outer place and stopped,
    With the birds still shrilling around him.
        And as if he could speak

He turned over on his side with his one year
Red as a wound
He turned over as if he could be sorry for this
And out of his eyes two great tears rolled, like stones,
    and he died.

Jon Silkin

For Chris

who died, 11th October 1987

You shall not disturb earth's air again.
Misted mornings, winds your music
on unknown shores and tides,
and I who love you –
mortal, berthed to earth
Cry Requiem-Kyrie
Kneeling in the leaves,
the wind torn debris of this
Autumn's passing.
Hold dying in my hands
the light of green-hazed Spring,
Summer turned for memory
falls sunset to the ground.
And all decays-decays
Cries Requiem-Kyrie.

You shall not breathe earth's air again:
Music of mists shall wind
your memory on shore and tide
And I who love you
come tear stained each night
Oh Requiem! Oh Kyrie!
and yet –
Love's day cry out
Luceat eis, Luceat
Light!

Vince Lively

Dying

1   Peace be to this house and all who live here.

1 & 2   We confess to God who is all Love,
Father, Son, and Holy Spirit,
that we have sinned in thought, word, and deed,
and in what we have left undone.

1   The God of Love and Mercy
forgive you and all of us our sins
and keep us in eternal life. Amen.

1 & 2   Our Father, who art in heaven,
hallowed be thy name,
thy kingdom come, thy will be done,
on earth as it is in heaven.
Give us this day our daily bread.
Forgive us our trespasses,
as we forgive those who trespass against us;
and lead us not into temptation,
but deliver us from evil.
For thine is the kingdom,
the power, and the glory,
for ever and ever. Amen.

1   Through our prayer
and through the laying on of these hands,
may the Holy Spirit,
the Giver of all life and healing,
fill you, N, with light and love,
and make you whole;
through Jesus Christ our Saviour. Amen.

Through this holy anointing
and through God's great love for you,
may the Holy Spirit

move in the depths of your being, N,
to make you whole and holy;
and may you be consecrated to God anew,
now and for eternity. Amen.

N,
go forth upon your journey from this world,
in the name of God the Father who created you,
in the name of Jesus Christ who redeemed you,
in the name of the Holy Spirit who is
    sanctifying you.
May the angels of God receive you,
and the saints of God welcome you.
May your rest this day be in peace,
and your dwelling the paradise of God.

The Lord bless you and keep you,
the Lord make his face to shine upon you and
    be gracious to you,
the Lord lift up the light of his countenance
    upon you,
and give you peace.

And the blessing of the God of Love,
Father, Son, and Holy Spirit,
be with you,
giving you life,
bearing your pain,
making you whole;
may God bring you through the narrow gate
and across the great river,
and may God reconcile us all in joy,
both living and departed,
in the merriment of heaven.

1 & 2   Amen.

Jim Cotter

Prayer for Body Positive Memorial Service

January 1990

I ask you now to bring here,
To this time and place,
Whatever is the sacred ground of your life,
The soil where the holy lives for you,
By whatever name echoes in your heart.

And so we go to the mountain,
Where Moses, the man of God
Heard the name of God,
And take off our shoes
Before the burning bush of God's presence.

We go to the place where the Buddha,
The enlightened one, smiles,
And embrace all living beings with gentleness.

We go to the book of Mohammed, the Prophet of
    Mecca,
And remember that God is the Merciful
And the Compassionate.

We go the hill where Jesus, the Son of Man,
Stretched out his wounded hands
And embraced the Tree of Life.

We go, as men and women, to that time
When a human hand first touched us in love
And claim the glory of being human.

We go to that moment when we linked arms
With our brothers and sisters, hungry and thirsty
For healing and justice
And remember our boundless hope.

Let us bring *our* Holy ground to this place
And this moment
And make it our common ground.
And, as we have kindled the lights of memory,
Of Hope and of Love,
Let them be mingled with the stars of Heaven
So that they may honour the lives
Of all our brothers and sisters,
Men, women and children,
Living with HIV infections and AIDS.

Let us say 'Yes' to life
By bringing our grief and anger to maturity
In laughter and struggle,
Dancing and playing,
And in the making of love.
So that every one of us
Has a place to live a fully human life
And a place to die a fully human death.

Let us say 'Yes' to life
As we remember in love and thanksgiving,
In pain and in joy,
In sorrow and in glory,
All those who have died because of HIV and AIDS.
As we pause for a moment,
You may like to remember by name
Individuals known to you and speak
Their name
Either in silence or aloud . . .

May they have rest in that place
Where there is no pain or grief
But light and life and love eternal.

We bring together
Our thoughts and our feelings
Our prayers and our gratitude
In the words of Jesus of Nazareth
Who knew both the joys and the hardships
Of living and loving,
Of the power of evil,
And the triumph of love,
The dying in pain
And the gift of new life.

So we pray: Our Father . . .

Br Colin Wilfred SSF
(based on an article 'Remembering our Dead' by
Stephen Manning, Toronto)

A selection of additional prayers
which may be used

Heavenly Comfort

Eternal Lord God, you hold all souls in life: shed forth,
we pray, upon your whole Church in paradise and on
earth the bright beams of your light and heavenly
comfort; and grant that we, following the good example
of those who have loved and served you here and are
now at rest, may at the last enter with them into the
fullness of your eternal joy; through Jesus Christ our
Lord. Amen.

In time of darkness

Father in heaven, you gave your Son Jesus Christ to
suffering and to death on the cross, and raised him to
life in glory. Grant us a patient faith in time of darkness,
and strengthen our hearts with the knowledge of your
love; through Jesus Christ our Lord. Amen.

Everlasting light

Father of all, by whose mercy and grace your saints
remain in everlasting light and peace: we remember
with thanksgiving those whom we love but see no
longer; and we pray that in them your perfect will may
be fulfilled; through Jesus Christ our Lord. Amen.

Peace at the last

O Lord, support us all the day long of this troublous
life, until the shades lengthen, and the evening comes,
and the busy world is hushed, the fever of life is over,
and our work is done. Then, Lord, in your mercy grant
us safe lodging, a holy rest, and peace at the last;
through Jesus Christ our Lord. Amen.

From The Alternative Service Book 1980

Author's acknowledgements

I am grateful to the following individuals for their kind permission to reproduce their work in this collection: Rabbi Lionel Blue, Jim Cotter, Kate Gibbs, Richard Harries, Eva Heyman, Cardinal Basil Hume, Bill Kirkpatrick, Sara Maitland, Michael Mayne, Martin Pendergast, Lance Stone, Colin Wilfred ssf and Pat Wright. Cardinal Hume's two prayers were written specifically for an individual who had been bereaved; they were not written specially for this book. James Woodward's piece first appeared in *Embracing the Chaos: Theological Responses to AIDS*, edited by James Woodward (SPCK 1990). I am also grateful to the following for their permission to reproduce copyright material: The Ave Maria Press, Notre Dame, IN, for the extract from *In Memoriam* by Henri Nouwen, © 1980 Ave Maria Press; the Catholic AIDS Link for their prayer and the poem by Vince Lively; Chatto & Windus, part of the Random Century Group Ltd, for the poem by Jon Silkin from *Poems New and Selected* (1966); Charles Elliott for the piece by Mark Pryce, which first appeared in *Christian* magazine; the Hazeldene Press for 'Acceptance' and 'The teacher within'; the Motor Neurone Disease Association for the pieces by Ivan Mann and Ross Davis which first appeared in its publication, *The Golden Key*; the Taizé Community for the piece by Brother Roger, © 1991 Ateliers et Presses de Taizé; the Terrence Higgins Trust for their prayer. The selection of additional prayers which may be used are taken from *The Alternative Service Book 1980*, copyright © The Central Board of Finance of the Church of England.